I0560546

You Are Just Beginning

A Journey Into Leadership

JIM RIDGWAY

USN, RET.

zolly
house
press

Copyright © 2025 by Jim Ridgway

All rights reserved. No part of this book may be reproduced, distributed, or transmitted in any form or by any means, including photocopying, recording, or other electronic or mechanical methods, without prior written permission of the publisher, except in the case of brief quotations embodied in critical reviews and certain other noncommercial uses permitted by copyright law.

For permission requests, contact the publisher at:

Zolly House Press
Boulder, CO
www.zollyhouse.com

Disclaimer

This is a work of nonfiction. While every effort has been made to ensure accuracy, the author and publisher assume no responsibility for errors, omissions, or differing interpretations of the subject matter. The information provided is for educational and informational purposes only and does not constitute professional, legal, or financial advice. Readers are encouraged to apply their own judgment and seek professional guidance where appropriate.

First Edition

Library of Congress Control Number: 2025919174

Cover design by Zolly House
Printed in the United States of America
ISBN (hardcover) 979-8-9930546-0-5 | ISBN (paperback) 979-8-9930546-1-2 |
ISBN (ebook) 979-8-9930546-2-9

DEDICATION

To Sarah. For everything.

TABLE OF CONTENTS

FOREWORD

Leadership is everything and everywhere. This is a remarkably simple statement. It summarizes my lived and learned experiences. Look around the world. When was the last time you saw acts of leadership that inspired you or that you admired? When others inspire you or you admire someone, what emotions do you feel?

I'm so glad you have this book in your hands. Leadership is about inspiring others to expect more, be more, and influence more, starting with your mindset and made visible in the actions you take in living your life. And, it is the most important thing we can do every day as human beings.

Leadership occurs when you seize the micro-moments that happen every day to inspire someone else or even yourself to make the world a better place. Leadership is not reserved for those with lofty titles or positions. It is a requirement for all of us. The world needs more leadership now than at any other time in the history of our human species. Our current moment of evolution demands stronger men and women to step forward and show the best possible version of themselves - the ultimate moment of leadership.

Leadership, like love, is not boastful. It is simultaneously humble and proud, like this book, which contains a wealth of insights and learnings for the reader. I am honored to be a part of it. I trust that you will be inspired to become a better version of yourself by absorbing these pages and discerning for yourself how the lessons herein may be applied to your leadership journey.

Joe Rafter

Builder of Others

Founder of the National Football Alliance

PLEASE NOTE

There is a glossary and explanation of terms for those who may be unfamiliar at the end of the book. Many thanks to my wife, Sarah, for pointing out the necessity of understanding not everyone understands all things Navy.

INTRODUCTION

In 2005, after serving in the United States Navy for 14 years as an officer and aviator, I found myself assigned to Navy Operational Support Center, Tulsa, OK as the new Commanding Officer. To this point in my Navy career, I had been struggling to become the leader I thought I should be. The Navy had given me little direction or formal leadership education. I was in the mode of 'fake it until you make it' as I took over a Navy Reserve center with more than 350 reservists assigned and a full-time staff of 14.

About a year after I took over, I'd progressed as a leader and Commanding Officer. I'd taken the lessons learned during my career and applied them as best I could. I learned about being a leader through exposure to other officers and leaders. I took what I felt was useful from them and noted what I felt were things best not copied.

One morning I had an opportunity to provide strong feedback to a young reserve sailor. This sailor had messed up out in town and I heard about it from law enforcement. This young man brought discredit to the Navy Reserve, and I had every intention of letting him know how I felt about that.

That morning, I showed up in a manner I never intended. I lost control of myself and honestly do not recall most of what I said to that young sailor. Upon reflection I realized that I had acted, as a leader, in a manner I never intended. I felt like I had failed the sailor and the Navy in how I presented myself. I had hoped for an opportunity to share with the sailor that I felt badly about how I had handled the situation, sadly, the opportunity did not present itself. The personal aftermath of this event caused me to make a vow right then and there to never show up in that way again.

This was the beginning of my formal pursuit of leadership education. I am now very nearly 20 years into that journey. It was not the beginning of my journey into leadership, it was the start of my pursuit to consciously learn as much as I could about being a leader and how to become who I wanted to be.

My personal journey into leadership began in 1991. I had been accepted into the Navy's Aviation Officer Candidate program and was making my way through Aviation Officer's Candidate School (AOCS). The Navy had a good idea; use Marine Corps drill instructors to train future officers for Naval Aviation. This has been memorialized in movies and television over the years, and yes, some of what you saw there is close to how it was.

My drill instructor, a Marine Corps Gunnery Seargent, or Gunny, was a master at tearing down the layers of how we thought the world worked as civilians, exposing us at the core of our being, and then slowly and methodically building us into the officers of the future. Each of the drill instructors at AOCS had a different style, some were more in your face and aggressive, others, like mine, were quiet, almost contemplative in their approach. We knew if our drill instructor started swearing, that we had messed up for sure!

Near the end of AOCS, Gunny would gather the remainder of the class in a room and share some of his leadership wisdom with us. We discovered that he was absolutely hilarious and a genuinely nice person. Something we didn't see earlier on as his students.

We began AOCS with 44 candidates, at the end, we graduated 15. There are other programs in the Navy and military with this level of attrition, yet for an entry level officer program, AOCS was one of the toughest. The ability to simply quit was always an option as the Navy did not want officers who were not willing to do the work. The program and the drill instructors whittled our numbers down to the core that truly wanted this work and career.

Right before graduation, where we would be commissioned Ensigns in the United States Navy, Gunny sat us down and imparted two pieces of wisdom that became the foundation of who I was to become as a leader. The first was, "Take care of your people, and they will take care of you." The second was, "You are just beginning." At the time, I had no idea how powerful these two concepts would become in my life. I was so focused on making it through training, I gave little thought to the wisdom inherent in these ideas. As time passed and I was able to put them to work, their power became evident.

I always find it interesting that my first career was as a Naval officer and that the Navy provided me with little to no training in leadership. The methodology seemed to be learn as you go and hope you figure it out. I now refer to this as "fake it until you make it."

Over the intervening years I have had multiple opportunities to learn about being a leader. Either through examples from leaders I worked for, or experiences and courses I was fortunate enough to be involved in. I have read many books, some good, some great, some not so much. There are some I'll recommend at the end of this work. I find value in them and perhaps you will too.

From my perspective, leadership is, at its core, a choice. Certainly, a person can be placed in a leadership position, yet that, in itself, does not mean that person will be a leader. Yes, there are some people who have the knack for being good leaders, for bringing diverse people together and focusing them on a common goal. I have found this is not common. In my experience, leadership is learned.

Leadership is a journey. It is a journey of learning. We make mistakes, we hope to learn from them, and we move forward towards the next thing. There is no end to learning as a leader. We are never done. In fact, most of the time, as Gunny said, you are just beginning.

As I look back on my career, 23 years in the Navy, and the more than 10 years in the civilian sector that followed, I realize that the wisdom imparted by my drill instructor all those years ago became the foundation on which I built my personal style of leadership.

Keep in mind, this is not intended as a 'how-to' guide, but rather my way of sharing some of the lessons I learned during my leadership journey. Through observation and learning we will each learn who we are and how we want to show up. This will change over time, as it should. True leaders never stop learning.

I have organized my tenets of leadership into three categories. The first are the basic tenets, the second intermediate, and the third advanced. A simple overall method to describe how challenging I feel these ideas and methods can be to integrate into how you operate as a leader and as a person. Your mileage may vary. Some things I describe as advanced may be things that come naturally to you. That's ok.

The basic idea is that we need a foundation to build the rest on. If the foundation is not stable and solid, how can what we build onto it survive?

The tenets I am sharing with you in this book are not meant to be all-inclusive. These are the things I have found to be true for me in my personal leadership style over my career. You may find some of them useful, others you may find less so. The idea is to learn, to think, and to come to terms with who and how you want to be as a leader.

All the examples I reference are as I remember them. I have not added any color to make them seem more or less than they were. These examples are things that have remained with me over the past 30+ years of learning how to be a leader of people. I do not claim that my recollection is perfect, however I feel like I am passing along the truth of each situation. How I reacted to these may be different from how you might, that's ok too. We are all different and handle life in diverse ways.

As I have written this book, I have moved back and forth on what sort of thing I want it to be. My initial attempt was more of a memoir, which was not my intention. It then became a series of leadership lessons with examples from my own journey. I feel like that approach is more in the style I wanted to use. I want to help people along their own journey into leadership.

I hope you are inspired by what follows.

You are just beginning.

PART 1
THE BASIC TENETS OF LEADERSHIP

THE BASIC TENANTS

E verything begins with the basics. We must, as leaders, be brilliant on the basics. These are the entering arguments for any situation. If we are not excellent at the base level, how can we expect to build upon that foundation and have it hold up? What follows are some basic leadership tenets that I have found to be exceptionally useful for supporting what comes next.

I have experienced a great deal, all around the globe. The Navy really showed me the world – remember the old commercial? Join the Navy, see the world? Well, it's true! Some of the places I visited were not very nice. I wouldn't necessarily recommend them for your holiday plans. At the same time, I learned from every experience. I saw things that have touched me deeply. Some of them I wish I had not seen. The thing of it is, we are the sum of our experiences, these things we go through combine to make us the people we are. These things influence how we show up in any given situation. Embrace who you are and what you have seen. Even if you sometimes wish you had seen something else.

Where I have personal stories and examples supporting the tenets, I will share them. The intention is not to call out any individual. I am sharing them for the purpose of example and learning. I learned from these situations, and I hope that you will as well. The examples and stories I will share are true to the best of my own, admittedly fallible recollection. The reality is that how I recollect these situations is how they help me as a leader.

1 – Take Care of Your People and They Will Take Care of You

When Gunny said these words to us, they made a lot of sense. Of course that's what you should do. At this point in my life, I had never been a leader of anything. I did not know what it truly meant to lead others towards a common goal. Just over two years later, I had my first opportunity to put this into practice. Before that, my life had been all about me.

I arrived at my first squadron a newly qualified P-3 pilot. I spent more than two years learning to fly. Single engine trainers, then multi-engine and finally the P-3C Orion. My only responsibilities up to this point in my Navy career had been not to mess up during training.

Here I was, a lieutenant junior grade, at my first operational assignment. I checked into the squadron at Whidbey Island, WA, and was informed I was the new Aviation Electronics branch officer. I had absolutely no idea what I was supposed to do, other than continue studying the aircraft so I could progress through the qualification program and eventually become a Patrol Plane Commander.

When I arrived, Aviation Electrician's Mate First Class (AE1) Smith, the leading petty officer of the shop I was now 'in charge' of showed me around and introduced me to the rest of the team. He was an experienced sailor with years under his belt. This talented, understanding petty officer would help me a great deal during this first assignment. It was obvious to me from the start that he had the experience and knowledge to ensure I would succeed in this new role. One of the first things I did was pull him aside to have a quiet conversation. I still recall exactly what I said to him. "Petty Officer Smith, I have no idea what you do here. You know this work and I don't. If you need me to sign something, please put it in front of me and I will. If you need me to learn something, please teach it to me so I can support the work of the team. This is your shop, not mine. I must study so I can upgrade as a pilot, if you need me, I'll be right over here at my desk."

As I was saying this to him, I was recalling the two pieces of wisdom that Gunny had imparted. I felt like I was taking care of the team by not attempting to impose myself into their process. I wanted to ensure they had what they needed, at the same time I also recognized I had no idea what that was. I was also letting him know that I had no intention of 'owning' the shop. These were his people; I was his boss for the time being. He knew what to do and how to do it, I had no idea. By being clear and concise about how I was going to operate with him, he knew that I was not there to interfere, I was there to support his work. I was taking care of the team.

Gunny's lesson was driven home to me a few days later. The Avionics shop leading petty officer approached me and said, "Sir, can you be our branch officer?" Another newly assigned officer had been given that shop to lead and he went in like a bull in a china shop. He wanted to let the team know that he was going to drive them toward success his way. I learned in that moment that the advice I had been given was extremely valuable. I had entered this first leadership assignment with Gunny's advice at the front of my mind. The word got around faster than I thought possible that I was being reasonable and easy to work with. I was taking care of my people, and others had already taken notice. I'd taken my first step toward being the leader I am today.

The success of this approach showed up for me in a different way a few months later. The leading petty officer and most of the team were away and it was just me and a third-class petty officer in the shop when the quarterly inspection was scheduled. I knew that my approach and working with this team was a success when the AE shop was awarded shop of the quarter following that inspection. I still felt I had very little knowledge of the inner workings of this maintenance shop I was notionally in charge of, however by taking care of the team, they were ensuring I looked good when the squadron leadership looked at me.

The other thing that hit me like a ton of bricks was that I truly was just beginning. I felt completely overwhelmed by the operations going on around me. It was foreign to me as I just did not know how things worked at the squadron and had no real idea what was expected of me. This was my first experience with how the Navy, in my experience, developed leaders. I was thrown into the deep end to see if I could swim. It was awesomely uncomfortable, and it felt like a heavy burden.

Sometime later I was given a new assignment in that first squadron. I took Gunny's advice with me each time I moved on. To this day, it has never failed me. Taking care of those who report to you is a basic tenet of being a leader. If your team is not well supported, they will not be able to perform as needed by the organization. They will feel like they are not valued, and they will move on to another organization in the hope they will find what they need. By taking care of your team, you are showing them you care about them as people. You don't have to get personal; the idea is to support them in what they do every step of the way. Through support and trust that they know what they are doing, you show the value they bring to the team and organization.

2 – Transparency Builds Trust

Transparency builds trust. On the surface, this simple statement seems to be common sense. At the same time everyone I know has examples of times where their leadership was not transparent. Trust is like a bank account. If you make deposits of trust, then you have a balance. If you only make deposits, you will become wealthy with trust by your team. They will not doubt you, and they will support you because they trust that you are leading them in the right direction, even if that direction does not make complete sense to them in the moment.

We want our teams to support what we decide. We must ensure they trust what we are saying to garner that support. If we fail at trust, we will fail as leaders. The team that does not trust their leaders will not support their efforts. When leaders are not trusted, they cannot call upon the team to go the extra mile to ensure success. So much that supports success is built on trust. How can we expect our teams to back us, even when they do not fully understand the end state, if we are not trusted?

When I arrived at the Navy Operational Support Center (NOSC) in Tulsa, OK as the new Commanding Officer (CO), I found a team of consummate professionals who had a very low level of trust in leadership. I set about learning what I could about the command and making my rounds each day, visiting each of the offices and just getting to know the team. I've sometimes heard this referred to as management by walking around.

One morning, I walked into the supply department and the leading petty officer stood up and asked, "Sir, what's the matter?" She appeared alarmed and I quickly assured her that I was just there to see how things were going and to see if she needed my support on anything. She answered me by stating that the previous CO had only come into the supply department one time during his tenure and that was to yell at her.

For those unfamiliar with the Navy Reserve, the part-time enlisted and officers come into a reserve center or unit once per month for the weekend. They work Saturday and Sunday to get credit for their service. Additionally, they must each spend at least two weeks per year in Active Training where they go on active duty to support their regular Navy units. We call the time when they come into the NOSC "drill weekends."

After the first drill weekend at NOSC Tulsa, I invited the leadership of the various reserve units into my office at the end of the Sunday. They trickled in and I asked them all to sit down so we could do a 'hot washup' on what went well that weekend and where things could improve. My role was to support these reservists and their units, ensure they were paid on time, and all their administrative issues were dealt with.

I was surprised to initially have this invitation met with skepticism. When I asked why this was, a couple of the unit COs mentioned they had never been in the NOSC COs office before. In fact, he had rarely ventured out of his office to visit with the units and see how they were doing during the drill weekends. I assured them all I was there to support them, in fact that was my job, any and all feedback would be accepted and acted upon.

In both cases, I was being transparent about who I was, how I wanted to operate, and what I expected from the people I was there to lead and support. I was building back trust in the leadership of NOSC

Tulsa to ensure I was able to perform to my utmost and ensure the reserve units were supported at a level they deserved. I was making those deposits into the account of trust.

Then, there's the other side of the trust coin. Just as there are leaders who go out of their way to be transparent and support the team, there are those who actively hide their true intentions. I sadly experienced this situation two years after my retirement from the Navy.

My initial role in the civilian sector was as a change management professional for a large utility company on the West coast of the United States. The team I had been hired to support was a very high functioning team working to support a very old and established company. My boss saw how I could bring my unique experiences to the table and help round the overall experience of the group.

Just about two years into this role, I had already been internally recruited out of the team and was within a couple of months of moving to my new group within the company. Where the change team reported into had been passed to a different leader who had, in the past, been openly hostile to our mission. This leader had stated he did not see the value in what the change team brought to the company.

In public forums, this new leader indicated support for our team and mission. He then placed my boss under the direction of one of his peers of equal standing within the company. This was a very unusual move. That leader then proceeded to meet with each of the team members. I distinctly recall my meeting with him where he indicated full support for the work we were doing.

There is an old saying, "go with your gut." The feeling I had following that encounter was one of 'this guy did not say one true thing during the entire meeting.' His entire demeanor felt off and I had no faith at all in what he was telling me. When the team compared notes following our individual discussions with this person, we were all left with similar impressions. We knew that his boss had made statements about the lack of value he felt our team brought to the table, and we were now being told we would be fully supported in the work we were doing. The entire idea of us reporting up this chain of command just felt wrong.

The result was there was absolutely zero trust built by the new leadership with the team I was on. We did not believe anything they told us about the future of our function. We felt their agenda was to dismantle and remove the team from the organization. In this situation, the upper tier leadership was not open to feedback. We were helpless to push back on what was occurring and had no option other than to see how things ended up.

About two weeks later I moved to my new role in the company. Within two months, my former boss had been driven to resign and the new team leader began to systematically dismantle the group and their function from the company. The feelings of the team turned out to be completely founded. We were right not to trust them. The impact of their actions cannot be measured. The team was doing excellent work, some of the change projects we brought to the company are now embedded in how we do business. Who knows what we could have accomplished if given the chance.

The leaders who performed this move lost all credibility with me and I did not trust them one iota. The other, more senior leader had used his direct report as his hatchet-man to do the dirty work he did not want to do himself. The hatchet-man was eventually forced out of the company, fired for misconduct. I recall feeling satisfaction with that result at the time. The more senior leader poisoned all interactions we had in the future, and I was very glad to see him eventually leave the company for 'other opportunities.'

The reality is that leaders have a duty to be open and honest with those they lead. Being this way is not always simple or comfortable, but, through transparency, trust is built. Think of transparency as a large slab of granite or a solid slab you might build a house on. Now think of lack of transparency as soft soil or even quicksand. Which would you rather build your foundation upon? Even if the news you share is not seen as positive, when you are transparent with the team, they will trust you. If you are not, they will not. This is simple human nature. When you deliver bad news, unfiltered, those who must live with it should not harbor ill will towards you. Honesty is the same as transparency. The trust that creates becomes support. Even if it's given grudgingly, your people will trust you to be there when needed. These men failed in all aspects of transparency and trust. If I ran into either of them on the street today, I would not even give them the time of day.

3 – Walk The Talk

You may have heard the saying "Do as I say, not as I do", or something along those lines. The reality is, just like transparency builds trust, you must walk the talk you put out into the team. This holds true for all things from asking the team to perform something unpleasant to ensuring everyone follows safety guidelines. If the leader does not model the behavior they are seeking, the team will not either.

In my current role in the civilian sector, I run a team of emergency management professionals. This team monitors the entire service territory of more than 70,000 square miles for hazards that could impact company assets. These impacts can have disastrous effects. For example, if our assets start a major fire, we would be held accountable. If there is a major natural disaster, the team provides critical information to the rest of the organization enabling them to respond appropriately to the disaster. One of the things that comes along with this job is supporting the emergency team when bad things happen.

This may require working more days in a row than people would like. They have families and other commitments, and most of the team came out of the first responder world, so their desire to work more than five or six days in a row was, understandably, low.

In 2021 we had a major incident impact the company. This incident and our response to it ran for three months. Our emergency operations center was active for much of that time to handle our response to the incident. My team has a representative in the emergency operations center whenever it is activated. I knew that this was going to be a long-haul response and that my team was busy handling the asks for information that were coming in from all sides.

I took the opportunity to Walk the Talk in that moment. I purposely took on the role as the representative for my team, working 12 to14-hour days, for 26 days straight. I wanted to show the team that I would not ask them to do anything I was not willing to do myself. I also wanted to show the team we would support emergency efforts wherever and whenever we were needed. Leading the charge on that incident, early in my tenure, showed the team I was serious about our mission, and I was willing to put myself into the hot seat for an extended period. That way, if I asked one of them to do the same, there could be no realistic push back on the need.

During my time in the Navy, we were often under a great deal of pressure to get things done quickly, and properly. I made it a point to review the message traffic each morning to see what other units had reported and how I could use those lessons to help my team.

In the Navy, one of the most high-profile roles in the squadron is being the officer in charge of aircraft maintenance. Military aviation is excellent at telling on itself. We would send hazard reports anytime something went awry so that others could learn from what happened. Early one morning, while I was the maintenance officer at my last squadron, I read a message that a sister squadron sent. They also flew the P-3C Orion aircraft that we were operating. The maintenance processes and procedures were the same for all squadrons and there was zero wiggle room for going off and doing something different. The expectation was always, do it by the book, every time, no exceptions.

By the book, every time, no exceptions became my mantra during the time I was flying. The expressed expectations (the Talk) were well documented and there was no excuse for not following the process. Yet pressure to perform and complete tasks is very real. The squadron that sent the message had an incident that they felt needed to be shared with all other squadrons.

Their overnight aircraft maintenance team did some work on an aircraft that required the plane to be flown to ensure the issue had been corrected. The technician completed the work and submitted it to the quality control inspector for final signoff. That Quality Assurance (QA) team member knew the technician, felt confident they had done the work properly, and signed off on the repair without inspecting the work. They most certainly felt pressure to get the aircraft back into an operational status and just wanted to get it done. This is what is known as 'gun-decking' or 'pencil-whipping', the inspector simply trusted the worker without verifying the work.

The next morning the crew assigned to test fly the aircraft did their preflight and got ready to take off. As they were rolling down the runway, the pilot at the controls felt something was not right and aborted the takeoff. They came to a stop, turned around and did a high-speed taxi back to the takeoff position with the co-pilot at the controls to see if they felt anything was wrong. The co-pilot did not feel there was anything amiss, so they started the takeoff roll again, and again, the pilot aborted the takeoff. They taxied the aircraft back and had it inspected.

The inspection revealed that the maintenance work required the disconnection of one of the ailerons on the plane. When the work was complete, the parts were put back together, however the bolt that held the pieces together was not replaced. This caused the parts to separate during the takeoff roll and the feeling of something not right for the pilot. The ensuing investigation revealed the QA inspector's error in not inspecting the work as required.

I used this incident as a lesson for my team. There was nothing so important that the QA team could not perform their work properly. If there was a couple of hours delay, it was not a big deal, except in the mind of that 'can-do' person who felt it had to get done right then. That person held others to the standard of the procedures and expected them to perform perfectly, every time. In this instance, the QA inspector allowed the pressure to get the job signed off get in the way of doing the job correctly. They failed to double-check a critical safety item, and who knows what would have occurred had that aircraft become airborne. The pilots may have been able to control the aircraft with just one aileron functioning. They also may not have been able to control it with just one aileron. Fortunately, they did not have to find out.

When I asked my aviation maintenance team how much they thought the aircrew team at that other squadron trusted their maintenance team, they answered 'not much'. This is the point of the lesson. When we expect performance to a standard, we must hold ourselves to that very same, if not a higher standard. We must Walk the Talk.

Walking the talk is a part of the foundation for good leadership. From creating a safe space, to ensuring transparency, to supporting team members who desire to move to a new role. If the leaders do not Walk the Talk, the team will be far less likely to support them when needed most. Leadership must be the role model for all policies and direction. What applies to one, applies to all. No matter what the title on your door says.

4 – You are Not the Smartest Person in the Room

Coming up in your field and being placed in a leadership role can feel great. You feel validated that you have what it takes to succeed in your chosen career. You are now in a position of authority and others must listen to what you say. Why? Because you're in charge now!

The reality is that unless you are a unique individual who has knowledge and experience that absolutely no one else on your team has regarding the work you are all doing together, then you are very likely not all that. It really is time to get comfortable with the fact that you have other people on your team for a reason. They are bringing experience, knowledge and expertise to the table. Why else would you have hired them?

Our ego will tell us we know the answer. This is a trap. We did not get to a position of leadership simply through the force of our ego. The ability to be open to other perspectives, to thrive in a space where you are uncomfortable, to allow others to influence you with their own experience is essential. This is a large part of what being a leader means. You must be able to listen to, evaluate, and decide based on all that information and input from those who are the smartest person in the room in their specific area.

Being open to the perspectives of others is the basis of being interdependent. This idea is useful in all areas of business. It's important to note that this is not 'checking in with everyone before you do anything.' This is being open to alternate perspectives. This is being accepting of other people's ideas on the matter at hand. It is not that you must accept that perspective or idea, it is that you should be open to hearing it and evaluating the thoughts and ideas being presented. The ability to see the issues you are facing from multiple directions and perspectives will enable you to view how what you are doing may impact others. At the same time, you may just find a great idea that you had not considered.

While I was stationed in the New Orleans area at a P-3 squadron, I was the designated functional check pilot for the day, and the maintenance team had completed the repairs on an aircraft and wanted me to take it up and ensure everything was as it should be. The weather for a functional check flight is required to be what is called VFR or visual flight rules. This basically means that if all the instrumentation were to fail, you would still be able to navigate back to the airfield by sight.

The weather that day was not ideal for a functional check flight. As the pilot in command, it was my decision whether to take the plane up and complete the flight. The maintenance officer was eager to put this one behind him and get the check completed. In the end I decided to not fly that day due to the thunderstorm buildups around the field.

The maintenance officer asked to see me in a separate room and proceeded to let me know that he knew I just didn't want to fly that day, and he knew the weather was fine and I should just do the flight. He felt he knew what was right and that he could make the decision for me. While I appreciated his perspective, he felt he was the smartest person in the room at that moment. I very strongly let him know that I was the one who had to sign for the aircraft and that I was not going to fly the flight. In my professional opinion, the conditions were not correct, and it was not his call to make.

This was the first and only time I ever became angry at a fellow officer. It was not that he was wrong and I was right. It was his presentation of the issue to me, an officer two grades higher than him in rank, and his assumptions about why I was making the decision I was making. I considered the conditions carefully as I did for every event. I made the call, and I stuck by it. He felt he knew better. This situation did not endear him to me at all, and our relationship for the remainder of my time at that squadron was cool, yet professional. His assertions met with his desires, and he felt he could override me. The reality was it was entirely my call to make, and I was not going to be swayed by his desire to complete the maintenance check.

Situations like this one happen. Either you or someone else will feel they know the right answer and won't want to budge. The lesson here is being open to the perspectives of others and making the determination as to whether you want to accept that perspective. As leaders we are the decision makers. We must weigh the inputs and make the call. It is not always easy or simple.

When I left the role of Electronics Branch officer in my first squadron, I was assigned as the Educational Services Officer or ESO. This was a role that held a huge amount of responsibility and had great potential for scuttling your career if not performed properly. The Navy advancement exams for enlisted sailors is a very serious business. As the

ESO I was responsible for ordering, receiving, safely storing and administering the advancement examinations. These exams are a part of how the enlisted sailors in the Navy get promoted.

Just as some of the enlisted sailors have to deal with classified information, so their exams contain classified information and must be stored properly to ensure the security of not just the exam, but also of the information they sometimes contain. I very quickly realized that the chief petty officer (CPO or Chief) and the second-class petty officer who maintained continuity in the ESO office were far more knowledgeable than I ever would be regarding the process for Navy advancement exams. I also had the extreme good fortune that they were both superb at their jobs and took me in hand to ensure we all succeeded in our role.

I ran several cycles of the Navy advancement exam for my squadron, and we did well. I learned a great deal and the team kept me out of trouble. I trusted my experts and soon enough it was time for me to learn a new role within the squadron and I was to turn over the ESO job to a newer officer in the squadron. This occurred while we were on deployment (a squadron will deploy overseas six months out of every 18 or so) and I was informed the new officer would be taking over while I was away from the main site.

I went into this role with the same attitude I had when I first arrived at the squadron. I didn't know anything about the process, and I was there to learn from the expert team already in place. I was most certainly not smarter than they were, at least regarding this topic.

The new officer went in much like the officer who went into the avionics shop in the maintenance department had gone into his role when I first arrived at the squadron. He went in and started directing how he felt things should be done and did not want to hear from the team what the best ways they had learned were. When I returned to the main site of the deployment, the second-class petty officer sought me out and simply stated; "Sir, you have to talk to him!" She then related to me that she had attempted to show him how this process worked and how they had it set up and been very successful. He overrode her and stated something to the effect of; 'Me as the lieutenant, is telling you as the petty officer, to do it like this!'

I did go and find him and explain to him that she knew far more about this system and process than we would ever hope to learn. I talked to him. Whether or not he heard and learned was not the point.

I was informing him, as a peer, that he was not the smartest person in the room in this case. He certainly felt he was. The team knew better. I did not hear anything more from the ESO team after that. I like to think that he listened enough to keep the peace.

When we expect performance to a standard, we need to learn. That is just how life is. Being open to learning from and listening to those with expertise, is critical to our and our team's success.

5 – Be Brilliant on the Basics

Brilliant on the Basics is another concept I first learned while in the Navy. The idea was to fully support our sailors and families to ensure success of the overall mission. This ideal is still alive and well today and stuck with me as I transitioned from the Navy to civilian life.

What Brilliant on the Basics has morphed into for me is slightly different from what the Navy espouses. For me Brilliant on the Basics is all about getting the basic work done, and done well, without fail. This comes down, in many cases, to administrative tasks. Getting things like timecards completed on time, ensuring your expense reports are submitted timely and correctly, approving items that require your attention in a reasonable timeframe. What I sometimes call "Administrivia." While this work may feel unimportant, failure to complete it causes problems that take focus away from larger, impactful work.

As leaders we want our teams to be excellent on administrative tasks. We don't want to spend time worrying about timecards or expense reports. We want to focus on the real work at hand that is moving the needle for the company.

The team I lead in the civilian sector is a team of consummate professionals. They have deep experience and expertise in their field of emergency management, and they inspire me every day as I work with them to help them keep the public, our customers and coworkers safe.

Part of this role is to write summaries of the hazard incidents they discover so that their leadership, and my leadership, if necessary, can quickly understand the situation. I pull spelling and punctuation into Brilliant on the Basics for my team. Not only do we write summaries, but we also have multiple processes that we update annually to ensure we are up to date with the latest information in an ever-changing environment that may bring new hazards our way at any moment.

If I have to re-write a summary before sending it up the chain or edit a process or procedure for spelling and punctuation, then I am spending time doing something that I expect my team to have down already.

At the same time, I hold myself to a high standard when it comes to ensuring I have done my tasks. I approve timecards, I approve expense reports, I turn around drafts and more as soon as I am able. If I expect my team to do this, then I must Walk the Talk and do it as well.

I have also been put in the position of having to remind people above me about these things. I fully expect my team to do all the administrivia in a timely fashion. I do so myself. We all know people who are not great at this. I have found that as people move up in the organization, they have new and more drags on their time. This means that things can start to fall off their plate. This is where we have to step in and send gentle reminders to those above us.

Many times, I have witnessed my boss forgetting to approve my own expense report or neglecting to enter the quarterly or annual comments into the system of record. This is not due to any disrespect or intention. It has to do with all the things distracting the person from getting it all done.

Failure to do this sends a message to our teams. It sends the message that these things don't matter. This is likely very far from the truth. The optics of not getting the basics done on time can have far reaching impacts.

How do we want to be viewed by our teams? Do we want to be seen as on the job and not letting things slip, or do we want to be seen as having an attitude of 'it'll get done when I have a moment.'?

In the end, we owe it to ourselves, our teams, and the organization, to be Brilliant on the Basics. The base work is the easy stuff, and we must complete it without fail and well.

6 – Summarizing Basic Tenets of Leadership

Moving through my career, I have thought often of the wisdom Gunny imparted to us all those years ago. I have worked to meet those expectations for my entire career. Taking care of your people is my guiding principle. Those few words, imparted by someone who led marines and taught new Naval officers, have stayed with me. They ring true in every instance without fail. Taking care of the people you have the honor to lead should be the foundation of your leadership.

Transparency can be a challenge. We don't always want to pass along news that will not be taken well. The thing is, if we are all in the same boat, then we can support each other through the challenges we face as a team. Being open and honest with your team is one of the investments that will pay you dividends. Building trust is a journey, it takes time and effort. Losing trust can be instantaneous. It only takes one gaffe or misstep to lose the team's trust. That can depend on the impact of the issue, yet it is in your best interest as a leader to make those events as small as possible. There are times we are not able to be as transparent as we would like. There are rules and we do have to follow them. At the same time, we can craft the message to the team to help them understand why some things must be kept opaque.

Walk the talk. Never stray from this tenet. If you are setting an expectation, you must model that expectation. By the book, every time, no exceptions. Too often leaders say one thing and do another. This erodes transparency, it erodes trust, it diminishes the team.

Being humble on what you know, empowering others to express their knowledge and expertise will pay dividends for any leader. You cannot be expected to have all the answers, lean on your team and you all become better for the success that brings.

Standard work is the basis for what we do as leaders. Do it well, do it right, and don't miss deadlines. Being the example for the team is spread through all we do. If we fail to follow the basics, how can we expect the team to do the same?

PART 2
INTERMEDIATE TENETS
OF LEADERSHIP

THE INTERMEDIATE TENANTS

Becoming something different, acting differently, incorporating these ideas into who you are as a leader, takes work. It is not a sprint; it is a marathon that has no end. We are consistently working on who we are and how we want to be as leaders. This is connected to how we show up to others and ourselves each day.

The first step you've already seen. The basic tenants are the foundation on which to build your leadership style. Without that foundation what follows cannot be supported. This next, intermediate section contains tenets of being a leader that, in my mind, require some extra effort. These are the beginnings of setting up how you want to be as a person and a leader of others. The work required will force you to begin paying attention to how you are showing up each day. Ask yourself if you are meeting your own expectations, and, if not, what must be true for that to occur?

We will absolutely make mistakes. This is all a part of the human condition. Our goal is to ensure those mistakes do not have a significant detrimental impact and that we recognize and learn from them. This is the extra effort.

Think of the basic tenets as the foundation of the building that is leadership. The intermediate tenets are like the lower floors built above that foundation. They must remain strong, just as the foundation must, to support what comes after. Without the foundation, the building cannot stand.

1 – Listen Actively

Have you ever had a conversation with someone where you felt like they were fully focused on you and the conversation? Like they couldn't wait to understand exactly what you had to say. This is what is needed for leadership to fully support their teams. And it can be a true challenge. We are smart people and are in the positions we are in for a reason. We have what it takes to perform at this level and lead the team! The challenge comes when we are in a conversation with someone from the team or even someone outside the team, and we have a great thought, yet they are still speaking or expressing their thoughts.

What happens then? We may interrupt with our thought(s) and verbally run them over. They see you as not caring about what they have to say, or they believe you feel like you know better. Either of these perceptions from your team will shut down the feedback loop.

Feedback is a gift. I am sure you have heard that before. I say it all the time. The thing is it's real! Without feedback we cannot know how we are impacting the team. Without being open to feedback, and providing our thoughts, openly and honestly about the feedback, we will fail to progress as leaders and as human beings. This feedback loop, of soliciting the input and working to integrate it where we see value, is where much of the work we do to improve comes from. But those providing the feedback need to feel what they are saying is heard. Understood. Valued. Through actively listening, we communicate that to them. We show up in a caring and empathetic stance. It enables the team to be honest and constructively critical. It's how we get those good ideas from the team and encourage them to keep them coming.

One of the things I have had major challenges within my adult life is being able to focus on the speaker and actively listen. I have had people close to me tell me I don't listen. I could never understand what they meant. I always cared about what they had to say! The thing was whenever a thought popped into my head prompted by what they were saying, I would just blurt it out! This comes across to the other person as not caring, interrupting their flow. Even though this was the furthest thing from the truth, it made a difference. When I was doing this, I was breaking the feedback loop, communication stopped because of the way I was showing up.

I have worked for over 20 years on listening. At some point I was able to see what I was doing. I also realized I was doing it in a work setting! I was determined to change the behavior and ensure I was seen as someone who listened. Sometimes this meant I had to write down reminders as thoughts entered my head so I would not forget. Once I've listened to and understood the other person, now we can continue the dialogue and potentially interject that thought.

Changing habits can be challenging. As an adult, when this was brought to my attention by my then spouse, I worked hard to change that habit. It took me nearly 20 years to get to where I am today. I finally feel like I can actively listen and be very self-aware about whether I am being successful. Whenever I notice the impulse to speak out of turn now, I suppress it and ensure I can recall the thought that drove me to that impulse.

At one point I was trying to determine how I started the habit in the first place. While I was working this out, I was on the phone with my mother, and it became obvious. Here was the person who had influenced me to behave this way. She has the same habit I was fighting. We are the product of our parents. I found it interesting as well that because we were used to interacting in that manner, neither of us saw the interruptions as an issue. It was just how we communicated. Or failed to.

When other people are brought into the mix who are not used to this 'shorthand' way of interacting, it can cause conflict or challenges. We need to be as aware as we can of how we are showing up for others so we don't inadvertently shut down the dialogue. It can be very difficult to change, yet becoming an active listener can become a real superpower ensuring those who interact with you feel valued and an integral part of the work.

2 – Are You Showing up the way You Intend?

How are you showing up each day? It's an honest question and one that deserves serious attention. We all have an image in our mind regarding how we would like to be perceived. Both in work life and regular life. This is the intention with which we greet each day. The question is are others seeing you the same way you are? Are you meeting your intention?

Part of figuring out how you are showing up is being open to feedback, and sometimes criticism. If you are not open to others sharing how they perceive you, how are you going to know?

Shortly after I arrived at NOSC Alameda as the new Commanding Officer (CO), I was in a meeting with my staff and had asked my supply leading petty officer a question. She began answering with something that was not really related to my query. I stopped her mid-sentence and said, "No, I want to know about this." At the next weekly meeting I noticed she had pretty much stopped participating in the conversation. When I asked my command senior enlisted leader about it, he told me she was afraid of me. I was taken aback at this. I saw myself as open and welcoming of feedback and just wanted to get the work done. When I had cut her off with my correction, she thought she was in trouble. Her experience of me was not in alignment with how I had intended to show up for the team.

I used that feedback to adjust my behavior with my team. I realized I was not showing up how I intended, and it was making the team cautious around me instead of being open. How I was showing up, even unintentionally, was stopping the information flow I felt I needed to ensure the smooth operation of the center.

How we show up colors the perception of those we work with and for.

When I was stationed in New Orleans at a reserve P-3 squadron, we had a CO who was a reserve officer. This meant he was expected to show up once a month on a drill weekend (minimum) and perform his two weeks of active duty each year. Some reserve COs would go the extra mile and maybe show up a few extra days a month or perform some extra active time. They wanted to have a feel for the way the squadron was running while they were away doing their civilian job and make certain the active-duty officers entrusted with the day-to-day operation of the unit were performing as expected.

This CO felt he needed to have a more hands-on approach. He moved his family to New Orleans and took a leave of absence from his civilian job. He even attempted to get the Navy to pay for the move! He then proceeded to perform as many additional drill periods as he could legally get away with and was at the squadron almost daily for his entire tenure as CO. These actions were unprecedented in the experience of the team. This new CO was acting like he was an active-duty officer, not a reservist. It upset the balance and went against expectations.

It is important to note at the time this occurred, when the CO and XO of a Navy Reserve squadron were reservists, there would be an active-duty officer designated the Officer-in-Charge (OIC) who was charged with ensuring the squadron runs well while the CO and XO were not on site. This system was changed in 2010, removing the OIC position from reserve squadrons and alternating the CO and XO between active-duty and reserve officers.

This CO basically undercut the authority of the OIC for his entire time on-board the squadron. He showed up as a micro-manager who did not trust any of the active officers to perform their work without his direct supervision. The entire active-duty staff saw him as someone only there to make himself look good and squeeze every possible cent out of the Navy while he was CO through extra active time and drill periods. It is important to note that the Commanding Officer of a unit has the legal authority to run the squadron even while not on duty. The issue with this officer was that he was going against the norm while at the same time micro-managing to a degree the team had never experienced.

The result: morale at the squadron dropped, the officer cadre felt untrusted, and the squadron's performance declined overall. There was little transparency, and, as we have seen, transparency and trust go hand-in-hand. By showing up this way. he was undermining the support that was required for him to be successful.

When a squadron starts to decline, it is noticed. When things start to go awry in the military, the CO is the one who typically bears the burden. This CO, with his style and what was generally viewed as poor leadership qualities, did not stand out as a good leader. It is typical for a squadron CO to be promoted to the next rank after leaving the post. In this case, he was not promoted. While those of us who served under his command may have seen that as a just end to this situation, it also lessened our satisfaction serving in that unit.

How you show up as a leader not only has impact on the team, but it can also impact your career.

When I retired from the Navy in 2014, I went to work for the largest utility company in California. I had the good fortune to be recruited into the change team led by an inspirational leader. The work we did together over the following two years moved me further down the road to who I want to be than any other work I have done in such a short period. One of the areas he fully championed was personal development. He ensured we had the opportunity to attend an intensive program that not only gave us a solid foundation on the change methodology we were delivering, but it also allowed each of us to do a deep personal dive into how we were showing up each day. During the years that followed, I learned how I wanted to show up, to set an intention each day, and to be a leader I would want to follow.

Fast forward to 2020.

During the pandemic, I was hired on as the manager of a team that monitors a large territory for potential hazards. I showed up for that team in a manner that allowed them to flourish. I achieved this through the utilization of most, if not all, of the techniques and ways of working I am documenting in this book.

As I write these words I have been in that role for five years. Longer than any single role I have ever filled. I show up every day the way I know I need to for the team to succeed. The hard lessons I am sharing here paved the way for this success with a high-functioning team of professionals who inspire me to be my own best each day. In a very short time, I will be finishing my formal work career. Having the ability to pass along the lessons learned over a lifetime of leadership; and being able to do it with a team whose reason for being is to keep the public, our customers and coworkers safe has been the most rewarding work of my life.

3 – Use Your Leadership Tools, don't let them use you

In 2005 I left my last Navy squadron and was assigned to the NOSC in Tulsa, OK, as the new CO. At the time I felt like I knew how to be a decent leader and had the tools I needed to succeed in this new role. I was the senior Navy officer in Tulsa. I was also the only active-duty Navy officer in Tulsa. At the time I felt the weight of being responsible for representing the Navy in a metropolitan area. I felt I had the requisite experience and support of my superiors, and at the same time it felt like I was out on a limb, working to ensure we accomplished the Navy's mission for the reservists who came to train at the center.

It was during this time I experienced what I refer to as my personal wake-up call.

It was 2006 and I was sitting at my desk at the NOSC when the phone rang. I answered and on the other end of the line was a local jail administrator. They wanted to let me know one of my reserve sailors had been arrested for being drunk behind the wheel of his car, but not driving the car. This is called actual physical control and is a violation when you are under the influence. When he was taken in, he let everyone know he was in the Navy, and claimed all cops were pigs, and all his Navy buddies thought all cops were pigs. The administrator thought I should be aware of this sailor's behavior.

One of the challenges of dealing with reserve sailors is when they are not on duty, they are not necessarily subject to the Uniform Code of Military Justice. So, I could not do anything about this issue in an official manner.

All of that in mind, I had the opportunity to invite this young man to come see me at the NOSC a couple of days later. It just so happened that his reserve unit Executive Officer (XO) was performing a make-up drill that day, and I had my command Chief Petty Officer (CPO) and the unit's active-duty advisory CPO on hand.

The young man arrived and was shown into my office, he saw the four of us sitting there and clearly was wondering what was about to happen. I asked him, "Did you get arrested? Did you tell the jail personnel that you are in the Navy and that all Cops are pigs? Did you also tell them that all your Navy buddies think all Cops are pigs?" You could see the shock on his face. How did I know these things?

That is the last thing I recall clearly from that encounter. It was at that point I completely lost control and began shouting at this young man for all I was worth. I was personally offended by his behavior, and I let him know just how offended I was. The entire NOSC staff heard me from wherever they were in the building.

The next clear thing I recall is the collected CPOs and XO of the unit telling me to breathe and they were escorting the sailor into my CPOs office. I told them to have him come see me the next drill weekend and I would talk to him like a human being.

Here's the thing, he never came back. He left, did not complete any further drills and was administratively separated from the Navy. My boss saw that as a self-fixing problem. I saw that as a total failure of my leadership. I was not in control of myself at any point during my tirade with that young man. I did not do him any service, and I did not do the Navy any service by berating him without control. He never returned. Who knows what he might have accomplished if I had not done that. Maybe he would have failed anyway. Maybe he would have taken the lesson and become a superstar. We will never know. I was not ok with how I showed up that day, and I made a vow to never do that again.

Anger is a tool in the leadership toolbox. How it is utilized makes a difference.

I can confidently state that was the beginning of my doing the work on myself both as a person and as a leader. The work I have done in the nearly 20 years since that incident has been life changing and life-affirming. For me it took that wake-up call to show me the beginning of that part of my learning journey.

There is another, earlier experience at NOSC Tulsa I would like to share. I had a reserve sailor who had failed to follow direction as required. The Navy has travel credit cards for sailors when they are on orders, and it is required for them to pay the balance with the expense reimbursement as soon as they receive it. This sailor had failed to pay the bill on time, even though he had been reminded multiple times. In an organization, failure to follow the rules undermines the authority of the leadership. This sailor had failed to follow the regulations, and failed to remedy the situation when reminded by my staff. So, I decided to take him to Captain's Mast.

Mast, as it is often referred to, is non-judicial punishment. The CO is empowered to review the facts and has a set of potential punishments they can utilize to get the point across. I had never done this previously, though I had witnessed it.

I was very uncomfortable with what I was about to do. I called my boss and discussed it with him. He made a statement that put me in the right frame of mind. "You have to do what is best for the command, not for the sailor." That point made a lot of sense to me. Sure, we don't want to punish people. At the same time, we cannot accept this type of behavior and allowing it to go on without consequence was not the right answer.

In the end I reduced the reserve sailor one rank. Lower rank equals lower pay grade equals this cost him money every time he came to drill. I made it a point to talk with this sailor every time I saw him after that. I wanted to let him know that this was what I had to do, and I still believed he could succeed. I was very proud of him when he was able to take the advancement exam after I left the command, and he re-gained his previous rank.

While the tool of punishment or negative consequences can be uncomfortable, doing what is right for the larger team is what is most important.

There are a lot of tools in the leader's toolbox. You will find your favorites. And now, I want to re-visit the tool of anger once more.

In 2008 I was based in San Diego on the staff of Destroyer Squadron One. At the time of this incident, I was the safety officer and aviation officer. Some of the staff and I were on board one of our assigned ships for a pre-inspection. Every Navy ship goes through a major inspection every five years and we were conducting a pre-inspection to help determine their readiness for the formal, major inspection.

Part of my education as a land-based aviator with zero shipboard experience had been to shadow the staff engineering officer around our ships to learn the ins and outs of how things worked and what to expect. My engineering educator was a bright lieutenant commander (LCDR) who loved showing me the innovative ways that sailors would have in hiding things around the ship. One of the other things he showed me was how to check electrical panels to ensure things were as they should be. The process was very simple, walk up to the panel, press the button, check for three lights (positive, negative, and ground). Shipboard power is typically 440 volts and can have a high amperage, so ensuring the wiring was working properly mattered.

During our pre-inspection, this LCDR showed me a panel that was indicating a fault in the ground of the circuit. He told me he informed the ship safety officer of the issue a week prior. I asked him what the worst thing that could happen would be. He told me, if there was a short-circuit, someone could be electrocuted--and potentially die. So yes, it mattered.

I then walked to the bridge wing of the ship with him and my force-protection officer, who was another LCDR, and asked the sailor on duty in the bridge to call the ship Operations Officer to the bridge wing. It is important to note that the Operations Officer is also the Safety Officer on board a Navy Frigate.

I need to pause the story for a moment to share how I had been showing up with the staff to that point. I had been at the destroyer squadron for about a year. I was relaxed in my role at the destroyer squadron. I was there to bring safety and aviation expertise to the team, and I happened to be senior in rank to the entire staff other than the Commodore, who was a captain. They saw me as a relaxed and reasonable senior officer in the command. I never yelled and swore very little. It was a positive assignment for me to relax a little and get used to how the surface Navy worked. I had no experience in this realm as I was a land-based aviator for my entire career up to that point. I was very open with the officers on the staff that I did not know what I did not know, and they took it in turn to educate me about how the assigned ships were supposed to work.

Back to our story...

As we were waiting for the Operations Officer to arrive, I was preparing to use the tools I had at hand to get the message across.

The officer reported to the bridge wing as ordered and approached me inquiring what he could do for me. I turned to him, and in a measured, and controlled, angry voice, said "What the fuck Ops! LCDR Casale showed you this malfunctioning electrical panel a week ago and it's still showing the malfunction! Does someone have to DIE for you to get it fixed?!" The officer in question replied with a very worried "No sir!" and I dismissed him to remedy the situation.

It was at that point that the stunned force-protection officer turned to me and said, "Who are you?" I turned to him with a smile on my face and said, "You just have to know when to bring it out."

The point of relating this situation is that anger is a valid tool in the leader's toolbox. It can be extremely effective. It can be most effective if you, as a leader, are typically calm and measured. The difference between my wake-up call two years prior and this instance was that I used anger in this case in an intentional and controlled manner to get my point across.

In this case, it worked exceptionally well for me. I used the tool. In the first case, my wake-up call, the tool used me, and I saw that as ineffective.

As you build your own leadership toolbox and fill it with the tools that resonate with you, make every effort to read the situation and use them to their greatest effect.

4 – Do Not Have a Zero-Defect Mentality

We are humans and humans are fallible. We make mistakes. To err is human. This is part of the deal. I have found it best to assume positive intent, and when the people under me make an error, I take the time to try and find out how I, or the team failed, not the individual.

So often in recent years we've seen those who make mistakes removed from their positions, without any real thought to the potential that person may have and how they might take the lessons learned from those mistakes and move forward towards being a better person, team member, or leader.

I am not arguing that all mistakes should be forgiven without fail. What I am saying is that if the person in question has good intentions, and they have made an honest mistake that has not done real harm, perhaps we could allow them the room to grow from that mistake.

People who do this are not defective, they are simply human, and I would argue most are capable of learning from that situation and becoming better. I've seen it happen.

The first example I would offer up for this is the story of a young Naval officer. While on duty, this officer ran his destroyer aground on a mud bank in the Philippines. This was the result of a navigational error. This officer had failed to check the tide tables, and the destroyer was stuck until the tides changed the next day.

Today, the Navy is a fundamentally unforgiving organization, had this occurred now, this would have been the end of that officer's career. Not only that, but it would also have been the end of his Commanding Officer's career. The Navy has existed in a near zero-defect culture for decades and things like this end careers. The officers involved are reassigned, fail to promote, and are often separated from the Navy.

In this instance, the officer was found to be at fault, received a letter of reprimand, and was sent on to his next assignment. What followed can only be described as a stellar career in the Navy. This career reached its pinnacle when he signed as the representative of the United States when Japan formally surrendered on board USS Missouri, thus ending the Second World War. The officer was future Admiral Chester Nimitz.

Imagine how different our country, or the world might be if Nimitz had been dismissed from the service following the grounding early in his career. The Navy was a different organization back in the early 20th century. The young Nimitz was able to make mistakes and learn from them. Today, the Navy is not so forgiving.

Personally, I also had the pleasure of seeing someone recover from what appeared to be a career ending error in judgement.

Before I reported for my last assignment in the Navy as the CO of NOSC Alameda, I was already briefed by the current CO regarding a situation with the civilian employee supporting the supply department at the NOSC. Apparently he had misused his authority to some degree, was caught, and dismissed. He did not accept the dismissal quietly and fought to retain his role at the NOSC. The case went before an administrative law judge and, in the end, he was reinstated.

The CO I was relieving told me all about the issue, how he did not trust this employee, and would not give him any work of consequence due to this mistrust. This had gone on for the entire two years of this

CO's tour. The CO I was to relieve felt as though I would be inheriting a problem.

I arrived and met the staff. I relieved the CO, took command, and went to work. I see it as part of my job to get to know everyone on the team. I met the civilian employee, and saw he was working as diligently as he was allowed to make up for his mistake. The two petty officers assigned to the supply department were doing all the real work and allowing this career Navy civilian to sit there and do next to nothing every day.

In my interactions with him, I did not witness anything causing me concern. I decided it was time to send him to receive refresher training on the most current supply protocols for the Navy Reserve and have him come back to work as our resident expert. He successfully completed the refresher training and returned to the NOSC. I instructed the supply petty officers to get him back to performing the normal duties that would be expected of a supply civilian worker at the NOSC.

A few days later it came to my attention that the supply petty officers were locking the records in their vehicles overnight to prevent the civilian worker from accessing them. They were not following my orders and were still in the mindset he was not to be trusted.

This was not the way I wanted this handled. I ended up giving the supply petty officers a direct order to allow him to act as he should. I told them that this person now knew more than they did regarding the latest protocols, and they were to work together to improve the team.

The validation of this decision came several months later during our command inspection. The supply department was found to have a model program. This was the highest rating they could receive, and they had performed flawlessly when inspected by higher command.

When I arrived as the incoming CO, this person indicated he would be retiring within about six months. Due to the changes we implemented together, he ended up staying at the NOSC, and adding value, for another decade before retiring!

I always try to experience first impressions with people without influence from what others may have told me. In this instance, it would have been simple and easy to just take the word of the previous CO and let this person time out and retire. I was able to give him a chance to prove he still had value to the team, and he continued to do so for a long time afterward.

Not all errors can be worked through successfully. As leaders it is up to us to observe, make the call, and see what the outcome is. Sometimes it takes time to see the full impact of those decisions. Not all of them will come out the way we want. The ones that do, or even exceed our wildest expectations, make all the others worthwhile.

5 – Leave Ego at the Door

Ego can be a real issue in many aspects of your life. While I do not intend to go into all of them, one area where ego can undermine your work, and life, is as a leader. You are accomplished. You have done the time and made the grade. You are now a leader of other people. You deserve this! Right?

I came up in the leadership realm in the US Navy as an aviator. There is arguably, no larger group of egomaniacs than military aviators. We fly fast, we fly low, we fly dangerous, we get the job done! The reality is your ego can kill you in that line of work. Holding onto the "I'm the best" mentality can, and has been, the demise of many. Military aviation is full of tales of woe where the aviator(s) just knew they could pull off this insane stunt or idea. The reality is modern military aviation is an extreme example of rule-based process.

The ones who choose to ignore the rules are the ones who end up "smoking holes." I was introduced to the term early in my career. My instructors would tell me, do things the right way or you may end up as a smoking hole. This term comes from what is typically left of the aircraft and the aviator when they make a poor decision and crash into the terrain. I am sure you can create the picture in your mind.

One prime example of this comes from when I was assigned to my first squadron at Whidbey Island, WA. This story is not one of a Navy incident, it is one from the Air Force. It seems there was an aviator at an Air Force base in Washington who no one wanted to fly with. There was an airshow coming up and none of the squadron pilots would fly the demonstration flight with this aviator. He was known as a daredevil and was seen as unsafe. The pilot had previously exhibited unsafe behavior and leadership took no action to stop it.

The incident flight was to be a practice flight for the coming airshow. The wing commander was the only one willing to fly with the pilot, and they took off and began the airshow practice. At one point in the flight, the pilot at the controls exceeded the safety parameters and the aircraft crashed, killing all four crewmembers.

The ensuing investigation called out several issues, primarily the pilot's "macho, daredevil personality significantly influenced the crash sequence." This pilot's ego killed four people and destroyed a national asset. Contributing to this was the fact he broke the rules and procedures multiple times in the past and there were no negative consequences, thus feeding his own belief that he was able to continue this type of behavior.

This pilot was not open to the feedback of his fellow pilots. Thinking about the fact that none of the regular pilots would fly with him was a massive piece of feedback, even though it was indirect. His ego did not allow him to accept that feedback.

When I showed up to my last assignment in the Navy, I made a commitment to being open to feedback from my team. I just completed my master's degree at the Naval War College, and I was really starting to understand how I operated as a leader.

As part of my check-in process, I asked each of my staff to come sit with me in my office to get to know them. I let them know who I was, what I did with my spare time, asked what they did, about family and their role on the team. I let them know how I expected us to operate and what they could expect from me. Towards the end of each meeting, I also expressed something that I doubt any of them had heard from a CO previously. I told them that it was 100% ok for them to come into my office, shut the door and say, 'skipper, you're all fucked up.' I then said that as long as that statement was immediately followed by why this was, we would have a great conversation. I wanted to make it ok for my team to provide me with the feedback I needed to be better. Trust me, this was not something that a third-class petty officer is used to hearing from their commander. At the same time, I wanted to change the way we did things so I could find out where improvements were needed without too much pain.

As I look back on that time, and with the clarity of experience, I realize that saying those words to junior military personnel may not have been appropriate. It has been pointed out to me, by someone I greatly admire, that I could have made better word choices, especially with junior personnel, to get the point across. This is wise feedback, and I take it as a lesson for myself and for the reader that I was and am not fallible. I acted in the manner I did in that moment. I used the words I used. Whether or not I was using them to the best effect is where we learn.

This meant that I would have to react positively to the feedback I was given. Feedback is a gift. Ego has no place when receiving it. Ego will get in the way of feedback. Don't let it. Allowing your team to provide you with valuable feedback will make you a better leader. Potentially a better person.

I still use this today. I used it with the editor of this book. Every new employee who reports to me or is on my team hears the same thing. I have found it to be immensely effective at reducing the angst some have around telling the boss what's going on. It has also proven invaluable for the leaders who report to me to let me know when I am slipping into their lane. I take that as the cue to get back into mine.

Ego will always show up. It is not an if, but a when. How we allow it to control or not control us is the important part. As a part of who we are, it will influence how we react to any given situation. How well we control it will influence how we show up in those situations for our team, and in our life. If we give in to what our ego tells us to do, we run the risk of undermining trust, we can ruin the relationships we have spent time and effort to foster. Being open to feedback is hard work, yet if we assume positive intent, and look to what is best for the team, we can put that ego monster back in his cage and move forward confident that we are making the right call.

6 – Take the Good From the Leaders You Respect (and Leave the Bad)

If you have ever worked for someone you consider to be a bad leader, you tend to remember it. The actions they took, the decisions they made, leave an indelible impression on your mind. You say to yourself, "I am not going to be like that when I am in charge!"

Poor leadership exists in all industries, in the public sector, in the military. We've all likely seen it. How we react when we are under poor leadership can depend a great deal upon where we are in our career at the time.

I distinctly recall being at my first Navy squadron, on our first deployment, we were having a good time. The group of us who were together as I recall were smiling and laughing. One of the people there made a funny statement, "I'm sorry, I'm with the morale suppression team, and we have to stop this right now!" We all thought it was a great joke.

The thing was it wasn't really a joke. The squadron's morale was low. The CO was demanding, not necessarily a bad thing-- and a micro-manager. When his time as the CO was over, and the XO became the CO, the change was palpable. The XO was respected, he cared about the team, he was very much a people-first leader. Or at least as much as he could be in a military organization.

One of the pieces of advice he gave me was to ensure I knew all the people under my purview. Even if they were assigned to a different area, and I did not see them face-to-face often. He wanted me to ensure I knew each sailor I was responsible for. How they were doing and performing. It was a great piece of advice, and I took it to heart. His tenure as our CO was very positive and helped shape my view on what a good leader should look and act like.

He went on to become a four-star admiral with a prestigious career. These are the people you want to learn from. Their success can influence your own and ensure you move in a direction that enhances your life.

When I retired from the Navy, I was recruited by a leader who saw what I could bring to the group he was building. I had experience running large teams, I had the leadership qualities and experience he felt was needed, and I had a deep background in safety from my time as an aviation safety officer in the Navy. He was extremely transparent and cared deeply about us and the work we were doing. He sensed that it was critical to the success of the company. He consciously hired each of his sub-leaders based on their life experience and how he felt that would add to the team. His description was that he wanted us each to bring something to the table the others did not have.

Having just completed a 23-year career in the Navy, I was unsure of what I could bring or how I would show up in the corporate space. I knew I had a great deal to learn, and I knew that there were expectations I would be able to lead those who reported to me to help the projects we were supporting to succeed. At the same time, I needed to learn the methodology we were bringing into the company and how to move from a command-and-control culture into one of coach and advise.

Thus began an 18-month period of my being very uncomfortable.

I was learning constantly both from my peers and those I was leading. I was learning how to apply the methodology we were expected to spread through the company to enable and empower change. I was learning what was expected from a reporting standpoint for each of the leaders I was supporting with my team. I was learning what was expected from my own leader.

My boss created a safe space for all of us to exist and learn. We were a team. We supported each other, we helped with projects, and we developed our own teams to support the efforts of change moving throughout the company.

Even though he, himself was not fully supported by the entire executive leadership team, my boss was able to keep us all motivated, supported, and fulfilled in our daily work. In addition, he ensured we each were able to attend a six-month intensive program that not only deepened our understanding and appreciation for the methodology, but it also included a deep personal dive for each of us. This was, for me, the most powerful part of the program. The insights into who I am as a person, how I want to show up, what breakthroughs I am seeking personally, were more powerful than anything I had previously experienced. This was a deep lesson in how I wanted to BE as a person. It most certainly bled over into my personal life and allowed me to develop as a human being and as a leader in ways that I will never be able to measure.

The level of gratitude I have for this opportunity is immense. The caring that my boss put into each of us was truly impressive. I learned a great deal from him and through him. He is one of the very few people I have ever worked for who I can distinctly call a friend.

All the traits he modeled for us have been integrated by me to some degree. Certainly, he was not out to make clones of himself, he wanted to enable us each to be the best we could, and he provided the tools to help us achieve that.

Contrast this to the leader he ended up reporting to. This person was on the executive leadership team and had openly expressed doubt about the value our team was bringing to the company. The results of which I have already described in the Transparency Builds Trust section. Actively being dishonest is something I will never do to my team. Experiencing this from other leaders has shown me how not to be.

Many of the sections in this book call out actions or ways of being that I disagree with. These are primary examples that made an impact on me around what characteristics I choose not to pick up from leaders I have experienced.

The truly inspirational leadership of others can have a real impact on your life. Being true to yourself and working to integrate the attributes you want to emulate is all part of the work to become a better you and a better leader. It is absolutely a journey, and it is never complete. Being the best we can, in the moment, is all we can ask of ourselves.

7 – Try to Leave Fear Behind

I discovered something very interesting about myself while I was at the Naval War College in 2010. I took the Meyers Briggs Type Indicator (MBTI) for the first time. The resulting output was a perfect match for the military – Extrovert, Intuitive, Thinking, Judging or ENTJ. At this point in my career, I was diving into learning as much about leadership and myself as I could. The War college has a core track, and I was also taking the elective track in leadership. Part of the preparation for this was taking the MBTI and seeing what the result was.

As I entered my second elective course, Self Awareness for Leaders, we took several different surveys and self-tests to give insight into how we operated as people. Part of that was taking the MBTI again. This time I looked at the instructions carefully and realized that when I took the MBTI the first time, I was answering the questions as if I was at work. This time I answered the questions as if I was at home, not working, not thinking about things Navy.

The result was significantly different. Extrovert, Intuitive, Feeling, Prospecting – or ENFP. You can go look up the types and take the test. It's an interesting experience. What I am pointing out is that I came to realize I created several coping mechanisms to succeed in my chosen career path. The Navy and being in the Navy was never who I was, it was what I did. I had become afraid to show what I perceived as weakness in my career. I felt I could not admit, even to myself, that I was not a great fit for this career. I know many people who were defined by being in the military. It was who they were. It was never more than a job to me. I was certainly proud; I am a patriot and value the years I spent in service. At the same time, I never let it define me as a person.

I came to the realization, 18 years after I joined, that I was far from a perfect fit for a military career based on who I am. This realization opened my eyes to something that had caused me angst and challenges for more than half of that career.

I started out in the Navy operating from a position of fear. I was nearly always afraid of failing at this endeavor. At first it was fear of not attaining my pilot wings. Later it was fear of not being able to operate the large P-3C Orion aircraft I had been assigned to. Having mastered those first issues, it morphed into fear of not being able to succeed as an officer in the Navy in charge of other people. The Navy, like many organizations, is very good at throwing its members into the mix with minimal preparation to lead. When it came to my core job, the technical training I received was world class. I learned to fly from the best of the best and then went on to train others to do the same. Yet when it came to learning to lead, to inspire, to manage the day in and day out work, there was very little guidance on how to do that effectively.

This cycle continued in each role I occupied through the first 12 years of my career. Constantly worried I would not be able to meet the minimum required to succeed in my chosen career path. I would avoid extra duty; I would worry about how I was showing up. I would pray for rain during flight training. This work life that I had chosen was hard!

The only assignment where I did not feel this way was as a flight instructor in Meridian, MS. That assignment was pure fun, and I did well. The team camaraderie among the instructors was excellent. I think that was the start of my emerging from fear and into confidence.

During my last squadron tour, in Brunswick, ME, I was given roles of increasing responsibility. First as the Maintenance Officer and then as the Operations Officer of the squadron. These are the two roles for a department head that 'check the box.' I succeeded in both and was then selected to be the CO of NOSC Tulsa. It was during my tenure as Operations Officer that I finally shed my fear. Learning to do that came through experience, good and bad.

What I've come to realize is that operating from a position of fear most certainly held me back during the first half of my Navy career. I did not want to go back to work after a weekend. I dreaded returning from vacation. Going into the squadron was a chore and I didn't want to do that chore.

I feel fortunate to have had the opportunity to work for some excellent officers during my time in Navy squadrons. Certainly, there were some who were challenging, yet I was able to glean some critical lessons from the good ones. I was able to see how a successful officer operated. I took those lessons on board and moved forward. By the time I departed my last squadron for my first test as a Commanding Officer, I not only felt ready, I felt confident that I would succeed.

I did not admit my fear to anyone during the time I was experiencing it. I sometimes look back in wonder at how I managed to get through it all. I would like to believe that it has to do with my character and willingness to gut it out and learn about how I needed to be to succeed. I think the reality is I had the excellent fortune to be able to observe enough solid officers and take the lessons they taught me, either through just being there or overtly, to finally emerge from my shell and take those first steps toward becoming someone I would be happy to be.

The years since leaving fear behind have proven to be some of the most rewarding of my life. I have been able to experience life and being a leader in ways that I never would have imagined. Once I was able to emerge from my position of fear and self-doubt, I was finally able to begin being the person I wanted to be.

It's important to remember, fear is normal. We all experience doubts; we all have fears. It is absolutely nothing to be ashamed of. The lesson here--don't let it control you. Work on yourself, build the confidence you need to become the leader and person you want to become. Not only will you feel better for it, but you will also be able to show others the way.

8 – One Answer Out the Door

My first career was in the military. A command-and-control culture by definition. You might expect there to be clear expectations around how things occur and what is to be done. There is a typical progression for the career paths of military members and the leaders of those people are expected to foster a culture of respect with a certain amount of predictability for the team.

One example of this is how officers are rated in a squadron. For my entire career, I observed that the goal, if possible, was to be ranked #1 in your competitive grouping, by rank, before departing for your next assignment. This would show you had progressed as desired and perhaps even exceeded expectations. This was particularly important for department heads as they were beginning to be looked at for promotion to full commander or selection to command assignments.

While I was at my last squadron, the leadership of the squadron was making a strong effort to take care of those of us who were the department heads. We were all hoping for assignment to the ever-shrinking number of Officer in Charge slots available in the reserve P-3 community. The P-3C overall fleet was shrinking and the number of opportunities had nearly halved since I arrived several years previously.

The squadron had already rated one of my peers as the #1 department head. This officer had been at the command for the appropriate length of time and very typically would be assigned to another unit while awaiting the selection process. In this case, the officer was held onto inside the command. This created a backlog for those of us remaining. The officer already rated #1 could not be rated lower without harming his prospects, the rest of us could not be rated #1 for the same reason. My fellow officers and I lobbied the command to move this officer on to create the space for another person to step up, and they failed to do so.

The answer we were given was they wanted to keep this officer in place for >>>insert lame excuse here<<<. The reality was the officer did not want to move and wanted the soon to be available OIC slot at the same squadron. The command supported this decision, and did not own it. They made up a variety of excuses for not moving the officer on. I was the next in line, I had my orders to become the CO of NOSC Tulsa, and I left the squadron without that #1 ticket.

Shortly thereafter I heard through the grapevine that the squadron attempted to move the officer to a local assignment, and were told by the wing commander, "You made this problem, you have to live with it!" While I felt vindicated that the squadron leadership was called out for playing fast and loose with the expectations, I also felt sad for those of us who were held back due to these decisions.

The command made a call, and the answer was obvious to all of us impacted. None of us ended up being seriously impacted by the decision, yet the overall dishonesty of the squadron leadership left a bad taste in our mouths.

The point of this example is that when a decision is made, each of the leaders in the room when it is made must own that decision. That's "one answer out the door."

There is no excusing it, there is no "I tried, but was outvoted". The answer is the answer. All leaders must own that answer. It must be one answer out the door. We can, and sometimes should disagree in private, but in public there must be a single stance. This goes to trust, transparency, and taking care of your people. Showing disagreement outside the space where the decisions are made undermines the entire leadership team. The divisions this creates generate distrust and can make it feel like the leadership team isn't aligned.

On my current team I have six leaders who report to me. We meet on a regular basis and there are some things that we must come to agreement on before we share with the wider team. I have set a process and expectation around this to ensure we, as a leadership team, are viewed as being open and honest with the group.

The main area where this comes into play is how employees are reviewed and rated by the team. There are expectations set by the larger company and my own leadership and peers around how we rate our teams. We must provide solid reasoning around the ratings we give our employees and, while there is no forced ranking, there is an expectation that the evidence for the rating must be strong. The overall organization we fall under within the company is very high performing so to stand out within this grouping takes more than it might elsewhere in the company.

As you might imagine, we can have some strong conversations around individual rankings as we come to the end of the year. The arguments are made, and the rankings are decided amongst the peer groups. I have my meeting with my team prior to going to my own peer group for our rankings, then my boss takes those results to her peer group and on up the chain.

At each level we set the expectation that nothing is final until we receive word back from the higher levels that our recommendations have been approved. We then await the final approval in the system of record after which we can provide the employees with their end-of-year evaluation.

The expectation I've set with my team is that we own the end results. Being a leader on my team means owning the answer. I let the people leaders who report to me know that I expect them to deliver the end-of-year ratings as they are with no caveat of "I really fought to get you rated higher, but I was overruled." This sort of message, while it may make the leader delivering it feel a little better, or even make the employee feel better about their leader, undermines the authority and trust of the larger leadership team.

The follow-on effects of undermining the leadership group's decision-making can impact morale, productivity, retention, and more. Owning the result, knowing you have done your best for your team, and delivering the appropriate message is crucial to overall team success. The reality is if you felt so strongly that a particular employee deserved a different rating, you would have brought the supporting documentation to the rating meeting and garnered support for it. It is a poor leader who blames the system. Good leaders must own the result and plan to engage more effectively the next time around.

9 – Be On the Barrier Removal Team

The first time I heard the term "barrier removal" was while I was in the Navy during my last squadron tour. The Navy was rolling out TQL or Total Quality Leadership and we were being shown what I now know to be some basic Lean and continuous improvement concepts. I share this not to tout the Navy's success at TQL or Lean, it was largely seen as a poorly thought out and executed effort. I share this to give a perspective on when I first became aware of the term.

Barrier removal is the idea that the leader removes the barriers to efficient operations. These are my own words based on my own experience. Your definition may vary. The idea in my head is that when one of my team encounters a barrier to doing their work, they have a short escalation fuse to loop me in so I can determine how best to support the team to get the job done.

This is where we must fight against human nature. There are many work realms where the leader says, "Don't bring me a problem without a solution!" In my mind, this is lazy leadership. I want to partner with my team members to help determine the best way around, over, or through the barrier to achieving the goal. I also want to be aware of the issues the team is facing when they are performing their work. I need that 20,000-foot view over all the work that is occurring on the team so I can see where some efforts may impact or help others.

At the same time, I have resources that my team members may not. I have peers and a boss who have contacts and ideas. We can all try and come together to figure out what must be true for us to meet the desired result. This approach can be extremely effective. At the same time, we need to be aware we will not always succeed at removing the barriers we encounter.

In my role as a change partner, I supported the corporate safety team. One of the projects I and my team were supporting was working to improve the safety culture at the company. Having come from a world with a very strong safety culture (Naval Aviation), I had a lot of ideas for the team working on this effort. I met with the director of the project; I assigned a member of my team to help lead the change effort and received regular updates on progress.

Fairly quickly into the work to support this company-wide effort, it became obvious my team member was meeting a great deal of resistance to the recommendations and advice we were bringing to the table. This person had regular check-ins with me and the trend showed a general lack of interest in how we were working to help the project.

In the spirit of understanding the challenges my team member was facing; I went to meet with the director overseeing the effort. Their view was that this effort was a project, and it would be completed within two years. I tried to help them understand that any cultural change should not be viewed as a project with a timeline. This was change at the fundamental level of how employees in the company viewed safety. I wanted to help the director understand my perspective on safety culture while offering to help with the effort based on my long experience in that realm.

The director listened, was polite, and did not want to take on any of our ideas or advice.

As I now saw the director in charge of the change as a barrier to its success, my next step was to move up one level to the vice president in charge of safety. I made the appointment, expressed my concerns, explained the ways we could assist, and the same thing occurred. The vice president didn't want to hear the reality of what this was going to take to implement.

In the end, my team made a distinct effort to assist the project team with their vision. The effort was a failure at the most basic level. There was a lack of understanding on the part of the leadership of the project around what must be true for success. As I write this, some ten years later, the company has made real progress towards improving our safety culture. The road to where we are now has been long and truly challenging. The company has been through several crises threatening the fundamental viability of its existence. Long after I left that role, the reality sank in on what it would take to implement real change around safety. I am pleased to see that effort bearing fruit.

Barriers can show up in a variety of ways. Recognizing the issue, being interdependent with your peers and contacts, and leaving ego behind to accept novel approaches can lead to amazing results. We have incredibly smart, inventive, and intuitive people working with and for us. Allowing them to move forward with their ideas makes us all better.

10 – Delegate, Delegate, Delegate

There comes a time in every leader's career when they move from the tactical implementation of their work, into the strategic direction of the work. This is an especially challenging time for leaders. We are experts in our field. We know how to get the job done. We know how to do the work. We have been shown to be excellent at it; thus we have been placed in this position of leading others.

Here's the challenge. Now that we are leading others doing that same work, we need to stop doing that work where it makes sense. Finding this balance is one of the most difficult aspects of moving up the chain of command for many leaders. We are good at this! We know how to do it. We like doing it! Why should we stop?

The reason is that if we do the work for our teams, what are they there for? How will they learn and develop into the next generation of leaders without the chance to do the work and make the mistakes? We can see the errors, or what we perceive as errors, coming. We want to step in and help, that's who we are. It's the wrong answer. If we do it, our teams will not grow, or at least not as quickly as they might have.

When I arrived at Destroyer Squadron One and was a brand-new commander, my boss sent me to several ships as his delegate to conduct pre-inspections for the ships that were getting ready for their major inspections. I had zero experience on board ships at that point in my career. I had been a land-based aviator for 17 years and never been underway on a Navy ship.

The Commodore sent me with the staff, all very experienced, to learn the ins and outs of how the surface Navy worked. He delegated to the staff to train me in what I needed to know. He delegated to me the responsibility of inspecting the ships and reporting back on how they were doing. I was thrown into the mix and had to learn quickly and leverage the expertise of the rest of the staff so I could perform the duties expected of me.

It was an exciting and new experience for me. I learned a huge amount about how the ships operated and what the expectations were from the higher levels of the service. This set me up for success in the role I was in. I was able to gain the experience I needed in a safe environment to learn how things should be onboard ship.

Just over a year later, I was designated the deputy commander of a multi-nation Naval exercise in Southeast Asia. My boss and I were embarked on one of the U.S. Navy ships and we had four other U.S. ships with us. We worked with six other nations during the exercise. I was there to learn and experience what it was like to be deployed on a Navy ship and work with other nations military personnel.

During that deployment, the Commodore left the ship for seven days for meetings on shore. During that week, I oversaw the U.S. ships as we transited to the next port of call. My boss entrusted me with the well-being of the task group. It was probably the most nerve-wracking time of my Navy career. I knew the CO of each ship would do the heavy lifting. They were operating their ships as they knew best. At the same time, I was on the hook for that week to ensure the overall mission was completed.

I am happy to say nothing out of the ordinary occurred during that week. I was able to learn from the experience and my leader trusted me to get the job done. He could have checked in on me frequently, he could have asked me daily how things were going, he could have sent me to the meetings and done it himself. In the end, he trusted me to do the job and learn from it.

When I started in my current civilian role, I was placed in charge of a team that is high-functioning and was not resourced as well as we needed to be. One of the responsibilities of the team is to ensure situational awareness during emergency events. Very shortly after I joined the team, we had several events where one of the leaders on my team would have to support the situational awareness needs. We had one event after another for several months. I jumped in, learned the role and what was expected, and represented the team. Thus began a year-long period where I was the representative for nearly every event. I knew the rest of the team needed the capacity to do the core work while they fed me the information to be passed along.

This period culminated in my being activated in that role for over three weeks. At that point, we were finally able to start increasing the staffing and garnering the resources and people needed to get the work done and represent the team. After another 18 months, we were finally at full staffing, and I began to shift out of the role of being the face of the team. I needed to ensure the rest of the leadership on our team was able to gain the experience of representing us at that high level.

Today, I rarely step into that role. When we have an incident where it is required, I am always an option, however I have turned into the alternate option instead of the primary. The team has picked up the ball and learned the expectations. They represent us exceptionally well in every instance with multiple members of the team now able to take on this role. The delegation of this responsibility and the trust we have in each other to get the job done has moved us down the road to success.

I have a fantastic boss. She has been in the company for a long time and knows a great deal about how things work, and who to talk to for just about any question. The organization my team is part of supports the entire company and we do it exceptionally well. My boss has held many of the positions or done the work of many of the positions on her team in the past. She absolutely loves the work we all do together.

This is where her challenge lies. She has been promoted to a level where the expectation is to delegate the tactical work to her team. At the same time, she is super excited about the work and knows how to do it. She is having a hard time letting go of the tactical work to allow those she has chosen to do the work and learn on the job. Seeing the challenge she is experiencing reminds me of my own journey into delegation. We all will likely have this occur at some point. We need to trust but verify. Trust those we have chosen to get the job done. Verify they have done it. If they have challenges or experience barriers, be available to assist. At the same time, allow them to do the work. Even if we "know" how to do it a little bit better. Otherwise, how will they be able to do the work when we are not around?

11 – Summarizing the Intermediate Tenets of Leadership

Listening actively will ensure you don't miss the point with your team. Being present will help the team feel heard.

How do you want to show up as a leader? Are you meeting that goal? Does your team see you how you see yourself? This can be crucial to your leadership success.

As you learn to use your leadership tools, make certain you are in control of them when you need them. Don't let those tools control you. Think about them as very intense power tools. They must be used with care.

As leaders, we have teams made up of human beings. Human beings are, by nature, fallible. A little understanding can go a long way, and recognizing fallibility can be a strong learning moment. Having a zero-defect mentality can have a strong negative impact on the team.

Ego has its place in life. Generally, that is not in your leadership role. Bringing your ego into the team leadership space will cause issues. Ego is the enemy of feedback. Being open to the gift of feedback will bring more success than having the shield of ego in place.

As we move through the journey that is leadership, we will encounter leaders we respect and admire. Take a look at how they show up, find those little things that make a real difference for them. Take the good from those leaders and strive to integrate that into your style where it makes sense. At the same time, when you encounter what you perceive to be a bad or poor leader, look at that and see if there is a lesson to be learned around how not to show up or act.

Fear will hold you back from being your best. There is no question about this in my mind. Being vulnerable is not the same thing. Do what you can to leave fear behind and strive forward. Find that balance between confidence and ego, where will you stand?

Leadership needs to be able to disagree in private. Have it out, make perspectives known and appreciated. However those conversations go, there will be a decision that comes out of that dialogue. It is incumbent upon each leader to own that decision. If we wear away at the leadership decision in a vain effort to make ourselves look better in the eyes of our team following a potentially unpopular decision, we undermine the work the entire leadership team has done to build trust. It must be one answer out the door. Leaders must own it, lead the team through good times and bad. Build the camaraderie that comes with a culture of trust.

Nothing can upset progress like a barrier. Barriers come in many shapes and sizes, from process to ego, those that put them in our way may not even realize what has occurred. As leaders it is our role to help the team overcome these barriers and move forward towards our common goal. Be a barrier remover, have a sense for how the team is being challenged and find ways to minimize those challenges.

Delegation can be a real challenge. As we rise through the levels in our organization, we must learn to delegate the work to those who are responsible for it. We chose them, now let them learn. We may cringe when we see them make mistakes, yet that is what is required. If we step in all the time, they will come to depend on us and may not find their own way. How will they be able to do the work when we are not there if we fail to allow them to learn?

At the same time, those new eyes seeing the work we have become used to, can sometimes find new and better, or more efficient ways of handling the jobs we have started to take for granted. As new people come into the roles we have had, they find new ways to see what is in the art of possible. Finding new ways of meeting the demands of the work can produce amazing results.

As we move through these tenets of leadership, we are building a foundation for our own, personal style. Without a solid foundation, we cannot build something that will last. Find the parts that speak to you, examine the parts that don't and ask yourself why. The idea is to learn and progress, continuously.

PART 3
ADVANCED TENETS OF LEADERSHIP

THE ADVANCED TENANTS

N ow that I have shared what I consider to be the basic and intermediate tenets of leadership, it's time to move onto the advanced. Here, there's less example and more learning. For some, I have relevant examples to share. For some, you'll see more of the idea or gist of the tenet. The best examples I can give you here are in how I show up as a leader and what has worked for me.

The purpose in this section is to continue to build upon the foundational work that has come before. The tenets that follow are those that have served me well for nearly 20 years as I finished my career in the Navy and began my civilian career.

THE ADVANCED TENANTS

1 - Never Operate from a Position of Fear

This tenet goes hand in hand with trying to leave fear behind. Once you have succeeded in leaving that behind you, it's time to make a commitment to never operating from a position of fear. When you operate from fear, you surrender your power. You operate from a point where whatever comes your way you feel you must accept it. If you can't do anything to change the circumstance, why are you even there? This is no way to be.

I have already shared how I managed to move from operating from fear to leaving it behind. I want to share what not operating from a position of fear is like. One of the critical points of this is to ensure your ego doesn't just show up and cast you in the light of being arrogant. We are already working to leave ego at the door. This way of being is to ensure we are doing the right thing for the team. We must stand up for ourselves and our team, period.

This way of being may not come naturally. Human beings are very good at beating each other down over time. We have all likely had bosses who undermine our authority and try to make themselves look good or better than they are.

My own first inkling of leaving fear behind and starting to operate without it came very close to the end of my first tour in the Navy. The P-3C has a crew of 12 people. We are a mix of officers and enlisted service members, and we tend to become very tight knit as we sometimes detach from the squadron with just the crew for weeks at a time. Interestingly enough our crew was known as the 'hate crew' and our motto was 'we hate each other, but we hate you more.' The Patrol Plane Commander on the crew was very demanding. He made the life of the rest of the crew challenging to say the least. Don't get me wrong, he was a solid aviator and knew his stuff better than most. His interpersonal skills at that time did not mesh well with the rest of the crew.

We flew a medical evacuation from Diego Garcia, a small British territory in the middle of the Indian Ocean, to Singapore. After we landed, late at night, he was demanding that I perform some planning task that I just was not up for at that moment. I just stood up to him and told him to 'get off my back!' It was the first time I had done such a thing, and I seem to recall I was just damned tired and didn't want to deal with his request. I would and could take care of it at a reasonable hour after some well-deserved rest. He did back off a bit and let me have my space, we went on to complete the mission and fly back as scheduled.

I don't normally think of this story when I think of leaving fear behind, yet I also feel like it was the start of me deciding to stop operating from a position of fear. A few years later, I heard this same pilot was at a different training squadron than I was, and his students that I happened to run into mentioned he was a great instructor. So, maybe he too had learned some leadership lessons along the way.

Later in my Navy career, when I was at the destroyer squadron, I ended up being the deputy commander for a large, multi-national naval exercise. This was to be my first deployment onboard a ship. I was still learning a great deal from the staff and the Commodore and I were embarked on the ship in overall command of the several month exercise. A Commodore in the Navy is a captain in charge of the destroyer squadron.

The staff traveled to Japan, and we embarked the ship. Each morning the Commodore called the master chief petty officer and me to his cabin. The master chief petty officer is the Senior Enlisted Leader on the staff.

For the first week or so, the Commodore would what I refer to as "Flame Spray" the two of us about his frustrations around how the deployment was progressing. The master chief and I would relay the message to the staff, at a much lower volume and without most of the frustration.

As this continued through the first week, and having been able to leave my fear behind me, I asked the Commodore to join me in a room on the ship near where the staff was working. I openly and with vulnerability said to him, "Sir, I feel like I am failing you." He looked at me with a small grin on his face, and said, "No you're not! You don't know what these idiots are supposed to do."

It dawned on me in that moment that the Commodore was spending the first meeting of his morning venting to the two people on his staff he knew could take it. We were his pressure relief valve, and we toned down the emotion and passed the message along to the staff. Being able to go into that conversation with him without fear, and the ability to be vulnerable around what I did not know, was a definite change for me and how I viewed my job and career. Gone was the person who was afraid of failing, and here was the person who was confident and able to step into the uncomfortable and face it head-on.

After I retired from the Navy and joined the civilian sector, I was in a new world altogether. I had moved from a strong command and control culture and into a role of advising and coaching. Having left my fear behind, I was ok in this new space. I was certainly uncomfortable; at the same time, I was relatively at peace with being in that zone of discomfort.

In my second role in the company, I was reporting to a new boss who had also come to the organization from a strong command and control culture. He trusted me to run the group, and I was back in a very comfortable space from an expertise perspective. One afternoon when addressing the team, my boss indicated to them that he and I were completely aligned on the direction he was giving the team.

The issue I had was that we were not aligned at all on what he was proposing. After the meeting, I pulled him aside and very clearly told him that I was not aligned with his perspective and that he should never state that without talking to me first. He had completely undercut my authority and transparency with the team by making the statements he had. I was not ok with that, and I let him know it.

I showed up in that case confidently and strongly in support of the culture I was putting in place for my team. Had this situation occurred during the time I was operating from a position of fear; I would never have spoken up. Reflecting on how I was showing up now made me feel like I was being successful in my role.

This tenet has continued to serve me well as I have advanced in my second career. Having the confidence to speak up as needed without fear of consequences has allowed me to model the behaviors I expect from my team. I am also fortunate that the company I work for fully supports speaking up. This showed up for me when I sent a very frank and honest opinion of the company's safety culture to consecutive CEOs. Each time they welcomed the input and perspective. Thankfully, we are finally seeing progress on this front, and I feel good about the direction of safety culture within the organization.

The other instance was when the COO of the company asked me to have my team provide some specific information for him on incidents. The information he was asking for was outside my team's typical workflow. Additionally, he had people on his team whose specific role was to provide that information. I let him know that my team did not have ready access to that data and that he was already paying people on his team to do that, so we would work with them to ensure he received what he desired, but my team would not be providing the information.

All these examples have, on reflection, proven to me that I was holding myself back for the first half of my Navy career. The fear I had did not serve me or the teams I was on. I needed to get past it and eventually did. The lesson here is to look at how you are showing up. If you are showing up from a position of fear, what can you do to change that?

2 – Allow the Leaders Under You To Be Leaders – and Back Them Up

During my final tour in the Navy, my Executive Officer (XO) was selected to become the CO of a different reserve center in a neighboring state. He was two grades junior to me at the time and was going to oversee a smaller center. The role of CO at a Navy Operational Support Center (NOSC) is sometimes challenging. You are the Commander of the installation, you make all the administrative decisions, and you must be able to stand up to reserve officers who are sometimes two or three grades senior to you in rank.

Once we learned the XO was going to move on and become a CO, I began an intensive mentoring beyond what I was already doing. I wanted to set him up for success and I knew he would be uncomfortable in the beginning having to deal with senior officers who technically reported to him.

An opportunity arose during this time where one of the sailors assigned to the command got into trouble. This sailor was not the best of my team, however when I reviewed the circumstances, I doubted she had committed any serious wrongdoing. The process normally starts with the chief petty officers. They conduct a disciplinary review board (DRB) and make a recommendation to the XO. The XO has the option of referring the case to the CO for captain's mast or stopping it at their desk and putting an end to the situation.

The DRB occurred and I could tell the chiefs wanted this sailor to be punished at mast. I took the XO aside and let him know that the decision to refer the sailor for mast was his call. The only issue was that he was going to have to live with that call. I also let him know that whatever decision he made, I would back him up.

The XO did what I needed him to do. He reviewed the case and came to a decision. His decision was to stop the issue at his desk. He let me know and I told him I would back him up. I also told him to stand by because the chiefs were going to be upset.

My Senior Enlisted Leader (SEL) came to see me a short time later and demanded I pull the sailor into mast. I told him that the XO had made the call, and I was not going to override that call. The SEL was upset, and the chiefs were upset. The upset was directed at the XO. I then told the XO, "Now you have to own it."

I am happy to say he did, and it calmed over time. Tough decisions are part of being a leader, and enabling your subordinate leaders to learn through doing can be a powerful tool.

Years later, as I lead a fantastic team of professionals, I am, once again, working to develop the leaders who will replace me. I have six leaders who report to me. They lead the larger team tactically while I try to remain more strategic. There remain times when I need to work in the tactical realm. That's part of the job on an operations team.

I try to live the tenets I am putting down in this book. This means I have set these leaders up in a manner that allows them to push on me whenever they feel something is not performing as they think it should. I have made it safe for them and expect them to act this way.

One of the things that I absolutely love is when the leaders who work for me show me they are being leaders. The main way this shows up is when they tell me to stop doing something that is interfering with that goal. The first time the team approached me; they were a bit tentative. You might expect that in a team reporting to a new leader.

They are working with someone they don't completely know yet and want to tread carefully.

The first of many "Jim, please let us be the leaders you want us to be" conversations occurred about 18 months into my tenure. Each time they approach me; I hear them out and I make efforts to adjust my behavior. Why? Because in each case they were one hundred percent correct. As an operational leader I can tend to get "into the weeds." By this I mean that I would listen to one of the junior team members who had an idea, and I would simply say, "Sure, let's do that." This cut the first line leaders out of the decision-making loop. I was making operational decisions without consulting the leaders who would have to implement them. This was moving into their lane of work and not remaining in my own.

Over the intervening years this has shown up in different ways. Now that we have established that I mean it when I say I am eager for their feedback and input, and they believe it, we have had several more instances where I have either nudged into their lane of work or been overly disruptive with the team based on my behavior. The adjustments have become slighter as time progressed. Typically, the leadership group would have one of them speak to me and I would take the feedback on board and adjust as I saw fit. The latest iteration really made me chuckle as I heard the same feedback from four of my leaders within two days.

This was awesome, because now they were all discussing any issues I was causing, and they were coming to me individually. I truly cherish feedback. It is the only way I can get better in my role from their perspective. Being open and ensuring it is safe to provide the feedback not only helps me, but it also helps the leaders who report to me become better.

The bottom line is that it is my goal to develop them as successors to my role. I have now had two careers, and in each I have worked hard to ensure the leaders who follow me will be as good as I can help them to be.

3 – Always Be Learning

Back when I completed Aviation Officer's Candidate School (AOCS), Gunny told us "You are just beginning." Looking back on that statement later, I realized the intention behind it. We had learned from him how to start being officers in the United States Navy. That education at the hands of an experienced military professional was just the start of our journey into leadership. I did not realize then how much more I had to learn. I did take his words to heart. I knew I had a lot to learn. Back then my focus was on learning to become an aviator, a pilot in the US Navy. I think he was more focused on helping us become leaders.

The further I progressed in my overall career, the more I realized the truth of the lessons learned at AOCS. The Navy, and life beyond it, continues to teach me that as a leader I must continually be learning to ensure I am able to serve those I work with. As much as leaders may like to think they are in charge, the reality is they are there to serve those who do the real work. Leaders create the environment in which the team functions.

Leading does not come naturally to most. Sure, there are those who seem to be natural leaders. Those who can convince a diverse group to focus on the task at hand and get the job done. I have found this type of person to be vanishingly rare. The rest of us must learn.

For me learning came from a variety of sources. First and foremost, as I have shared, I was set on the path by my AOCS drill instructor. The lessons he taught helped to create the foundation of who I was to become as an officer and leader.

As I moved through my Navy career, I saw good and bad leadership by those I reported to. I learned from the officers above me and from the sailors who worked for and with me. I learned from my own successes and failures. Experience in your chosen vocation with those you lead will provide you with lessons. I also had a strong wake-up call during my first CO tour. That experience set me on a path towards a more formal education in leadership.

I began to read about leadership. I enrolled in a distance learning master's degree course through a Navy program. That exposed me to ideas such as emotional intelligence and the leadership of people like

Abraham Lincoln. The books I was reading and the papers I was writing were helping me to place the experiences I was having on the job in a new perspective. I was starting to see that I had to keep learning in order to improve as a leader.

At the Naval War College (NWC), I was able to focus on leadership as my minor course of study. The courses I attended while a student at the NWC helped me become even more aware of how I was showing up and how I came to be the leader I had become to that point in my life.

After retiring from the Navy and entering the civilian sector, I had the extreme good fortune to start that part of the journey with a leader who was intensely focused on his team's development. The personal work I was able to do as part of my job moved the needle further and faster than anything else I had done to that point in my life.

Following that work I continue to read books recommended by mentors and coworkers. There is a ton of material on this topic in the world. I am adding to that pile. As I write these words, I am a 34-years student of leadership. I was not always aware of being that pupil. I was not always successful as a leader. The point I am trying to make is that in more than three decades I have never stopped learning about who I am as a leader or a person.

Leaders must continue to learn. This is a major tenet of my style. This is part of the culture I attempt to put in place for my teams. Leaders never stop learning. What Gunny said to us all those years ago remains true to this day. "You are just beginning."

4 – Learn From the Leaders Who Fail

Just because someone is in a leadership position does not mean they are suited to it. At times they are not even fit for the role they have been put into. If you are familiar with the Peter principle, you will know that there are some who are promoted to their level of incompetence. Success at lower levels does not always translate into success at higher levels.

I am sure you have witnessed this to some extent in your life/career. If not, you have likely heard of someone who fits this description.

Then we have leaders who are excellent, who are successful in their role, and fail within the organization. These are competent people who are doing amazing work only to have circumstance cut short their tenure. Some of the best leaders I have had the privilege to work with fall into this category.

Here's the thing about leaders who fail. We can learn from all of them. Whether it's a failure in general in the role they have been given, or a failure of the larger organization to recognize what a gem they have, there are lessons to be learned from each.

I learned a great deal in the Navy from those leaders I considered failures.

There was the reserve squadron CO I previously mentioned who pushed beyond the boundaries of his assigned role and into that of what more resembled an active-duty CO. Under this officer's leadership the squadron morale plummeted. This started at the top. The CO was making it exceedingly difficult for the active-duty department heads to perform their work without interference.

This was most relevant to the Officer in Charge (OIC) whose role was specifically to function in the stead of the reserve CO and XO when they were not present. This officer, a solid leader and officer in his own right, was unable to function in his role due to the constant interference of the reserve CO. There are other examples from this CO's tenure, but the main takeaway for me here is to allow those who report to you to do their work. If there is a need to redefine that work, then have the conversation and set expectations to come into alignment on roles and protocols.

This lesson is relevant for all leaders. We must allow our teams to be who they are. Certainly, there is far more command and control in the military, this does not mean that suppressing the work and morale of the team will produce the results that are needed. As I have shared, I sometimes need to be put back into my lane by the leaders I am working with. It is critical to be able to have the conversation and ensure the success of the team.

I learned another valuable lesson at another time from a similar dynamic. This time at sea. I was the deputy commander under the Commodore running a three and a half month multi-nation exercise. We were deployed with US forces to work alongside partners in southeast Asia to support and teach them in our tactics and procedures. We spent a great deal of time visiting and working with their forces to show partnership and cooperation both at sea and on land. The six nations we worked alongside were grateful for the efforts we brought. This was a high-visibility exercise, and it was expected that all participants on the US side would support to their utmost.

The CO of one of the five ships under the Commodore's command simply pushed back too much. He failed to meet the expectations of the embarked staff at nearly every turn. While I understood it was the CO's ship, the Commodore was in charge of the five US ships underway and made his expectations very clear. I witnessed the CO of the ship pushing back on nearly every request. Looking back on it now, I think he severely failed to "read the room." He felt he knew better than his temporary boss. This attitude trickled down to his own staff and their support was hit or miss due to his modeling of that behavior.

The Commodore was not attempting to run every department on the ship, nor was he trying to tell the CO how to do his job. The Commodore was directing the strategic work required to support the high-visibility exercise under his command.

This CO failed to understand the needs of his Immediate Superior in Command (ISIC), even if temporary. The end result was that a few months following our departure from ship, that CO Had a "change of command without the band." In civilian terms, he was relieved for cause. I never did ask the Commodore if he had something to do with that CO's untimely relief, but I suspect it was so.

The lesson I take from this example is to support higher level leaders to the best of your ability. There are times where it is appropriate to say that you cannot or should not comply with their desires. These are opportunities to have great conversations around expectations and management of them. By serving your own team as well as those you report to, the entire organization is supported.

One final military example is that of an officer who was brought in to be the deputy Commodore at the destroyer squadron I was assigned to. I had very little interaction with this person as he was away from the office for most of the relatively short time we were assigned there together. From what I could gather, this officer, a Navy captain, was fully competent in his role and there were no indications of issues with his leadership style.

So why he is included in this list of examples on failed leaders? A valid question. This person was involved in a very high-visibility scandal that impacted the Navy as a whole. While the details are not needed to understand this example, the lesson here is when we are in a visible role, how we conduct ourselves can impact our work life. Not only that, but the behaviors that led to the early retirement of this officer were conducted in his official capacity. When those junior to us observe how we act or what we accept from those wishing to do business with us, they will tend to perceive that activity as acceptable, turning bad action or actions into a systemic problem.

The activities of this officer and others was seen as totally unacceptable and led to a multitude of prosecutions. What you do and how you behave can impact your work life. The severity can be different depending on where you work and what your role is, but becoming a national news story cast in a negative light is not generally career-enhancing.

The next example of failure is more personal to me. This leader remains the favorite boss of my work life. He enabled and taught me more in two short years than I have learned in that length of time from anyone. He embodied many of the tenets I am writing in this book. He was and remains a phenomenal leader.

So why is he included in this book as an example of someone who failed? The reason is that the organization rejected him. He brought what the organization had asked for. He was hired to do the work he did. He not only did the work, but he did it exceptionally well. He brought learning and understanding to the company around the changes occurring across all business functions. He set up a world-class team to partner with the leaders of those projects. He set up trainings to spread the awareness and knowledge required to effectively deliver the changes. All in all, he did it right.

Then the organization changed his leader to one who did not feel he brought value to the company. His reaction was to keep doing his level best to meet the expectations of his internal customers and his team. He walked the talk. He stuck to what he knew was the right thing to do. Thus, eventually, he was forced to depart. He was not fired. There was no cause. He was performing to a high level. The leadership he was now reporting to made it so uncomfortable for him that he decided to leave.

This was a hard lesson for me to learn. I was saddened that such a solid and effective leader was pushed out of the company. At the same time, I was inspired by the way he reacted to all the things done to him and his team. He kept at it, he did not lower his level of delivery, he did his level best until the day he left. This was a tremendous lesson in how to be. His way of being is something I still aspire to.

Not all failures are the fault of the person.

5 – Allow Your People to Fail Forward

When is the last time your boss told you it was ok to fail at something? Never? I hope not. I hope the value of failing is something that is understood within your team and organization. The reality of performing at a high level is leaders need the next great idea. These ideas can come from the peers of the team leader and potentially the leadership of the organization. The best ideas, in my experience, come from the people doing the work. The ones on the front line of it all. These are the people who have to put the next great idea into practice. They are also the ones who can share what should be different in order to make the work better/more efficient.

The challenge can come in allowing people the space to try something new and accept the outcome whatever it may be. People, especially those who are high performing, do not like to fail. Making it ok to try a new idea and making it also ok if the idea does not work out requires a mature mindset around change and acceptance of outcomes.

The implementation of the new idea will require time and resources. Should the new idea not come to fruition as expected, the challenge is then to see where the value is in the attempt.

Outcomes of new ideas are rarely binary. Did the idea work? Yes, or no? Seems like it might be binary. Yet what were the expectations going in? Did the result meet them? In every metric? What did we learn? Is it worth continuing the new process or idea? These are the things that we must ask ourselves when we make these efforts.

At the very least, the team will know whether to pursue this course of action. This is learning. We learn every time we make a change. Whether that change is adopted is going to be based on the outcome. Can we achieve the buy-in we require to spread the new idea across the team? Should the new idea be proposed to more than just your team? Should it eventually be adopted enterprise-wide?

It is a complex issue. Enabling our teams to try things and then realize they did not work out as expected will allow them to grow and build curiosity within the group.

The team I lead as I write this has annual goals. One of those goals, every year, is to bring at least two new ideas to the table. I don't ask for them to be fully fleshed out on how to implement, I just want the ideas for the team to consider. I also make no promises to the team about whether we will use the ideas. The point is to keep the team in mode of continuous improvement. This requires me and my leadership team to foster a culture of curiosity.

During my final assignment in the Navy the command was inspected by our Immediate Superior in Command (ISIC) in all areas. This was a typical inspection that required them to examine our processes from top to bottom to ensure compliance with our programs. There were 72 programs inspected. For a staff of 25 personnel, it is a large ask to maintain 72 programs to a high standard.

In some areas we excelled. For example, our supply department was called out as a model program for others to emulate. In other areas we met the requirements. In one area we failed. The failure was in how we kept our records for the 650+ reserve members. Their training and pay records were not kept up to the standard expected by the ISIC.

My boss debriefed me on the results and when we discussed the personnel records portion, he let me know we would need to remedy the situation and have a re-inspection in a set amount of time. I let him know we were up to the task and would get it done. He commented that he appreciated my attitude towards this issue and that I did not push back against the results. They were what they were.

I worked with my team to implement the required corrective actions. As time progressed, I realized the team was not getting the corrections done in as timely a manner as we needed. I proposed the following to my team:

- Show me how to review the records.

- Give me 10 records each day to review.

- I would mark the issues I found with them, if any, for corrective action.

This had a couple of direct impacts on the personnel team. First, they appreciated the effort I was putting into their success as a part of my larger team. Second, and unexpressed, they were embarrassed that I was having to step in to assist with what they saw as their work.

I made no changes in the team, and we got through the records in enough time for the reinspection. I never had to look at another record after that. The team knew I would step in if needed, and they wanted to ensure I did not have to. The personnel office made changes to the way they worked with these records and were successful thereafter during my time. I accepted and owned the failure of the team. I had also worked side by side with them to remedy the situation. I had their backs, and they saw that.

Holding a safe space for your team to try out ideas or even fail at their core role is crucial to ensuring the team feels leadership has their back no matter what. In my current role, my team monitors a large area for hazards 24 hours a day, seven days a week. They are expected to find potentially impactful hazards any time, day or night. This is their core work.

On occasion something is missed. Either we miss an incident, or the indications of the incident were not what was expected, so we didn't know what we didn't know. It happens and it's rare. In each case, while I know the person who missed the catch is beating themselves up, I never ask who. I always ask what we could have done better to support the mission. People are humans, humans are fallible. We put processes and tools in place in an effort to reduce that fallibility to the lowest level possible.

When my people fail, the question is always what failed, not who. This is the core of the tenet. This is how we improve. This is how we move forward as fallible human beings.

6 – Hold a Safe Space for Expression

Holding a safe space for teammates to express how they are doing or what they are feeling is another key component to leadership in this environment. If we want the ground truth from our team, we must hold a safe space for the team to express what is on their minds. The key component in this tenet is repetition. When the team sees that it is safe to express themselves, and they see it again, and again, then we will begin to see meaningful interactions. Without meaningful interactions, how are we to know?

I first used this tenet consciously while I was the chief of staff at Destroyer Squadron One. One of the ships assigned to us experienced a fatality while they were on deployment. One of the sailors on the ship was killed in an accident during a major maintenance period while they were overseas. The Commodore at the time took me to the ship when they returned from the deployment and, while he went to speak with the officers and chief petty officers, sent me to the hangar deck to hold three sessions with the more junior enlisted sailors on board.

I knew going in that the crew morale was low. They had lost a shipmate and were feeling the impact of that loss. They came home and one of their teammates did not. I went into the hangar deck, where the helicopters would park when they were aboard. Without the helicopters embarked, this was a large enough area for the meetings. It was a good, mostly private, enclosed space where we could discuss what had occurred.

When the first-class petty officers came in, I very consciously removed my Battle Dress Uniform (BDU) top and hung it on a bolt on the wall. The BDU top has your name and rank embroidered on it, and I wanted to make a point. After hanging it on the wall, I turned to the assembled sailors and said, "Today I am not Commander Ridgway, today I am just a fellow sailor who wants to know how you are doing and what's on your mind." Through that symbolic removal of my rank, I was making a point that they could say anything in that moment and there would be no repercussions.

I repeated the meeting twice more with the second-class petty officers and then the third-class petty officers and seamen. In each instance, I made it a point for them to witness my removal of my official title and rank to reassure them they would not be in any jeopardy saying whatever was on their mind.

We had great conversations each time, and I was able to provide my boss with a clear understanding of how the crew was feeling. The interesting thing to me looking back on this is that I did not have a plan going into the meetings with the crew. I just did what felt like the right thing in the moment and it worked very well.

Later, in my first role after the Navy, I was re-introduced to this concept in a more formal way. My boss made it clear he was holding a safe space for the team every day. We could go to him for anything, say just about anything, and he would make it ok for us to tell him what we needed to. Not only was he holding a safe space for us to express ourselves, but he was also holding a safe space for us to learn the role we were assigned. Only a couple of us had formal experience in change management prior to taking this role. For the rest of us it was daily learning and working out how best to approach our internal clients to ensure we were giving the necessary support for the projects they requested our help on.

By giving us the support we needed and the ability to express our own successes and challenges in a space that was safe, we were able to find success in this role.

I use this same tenet in my daily way of being by soliciting feedback from my team and making it ok to let me know when I am messing up. Holding that safe space for expression and opinion allows the team to leave fear behind when dealing with me or other leaders in the organization.

Another great tool in this space is creating the ability for anonymous feedback to leadership and the team. I have created a feedback/suggestion box form for my team that does not require the submitter to add their name. I want to make sure I get all their good ideas and feedback, even if they are not yet comfortable giving it face to face. The interesting thing is, about 95% of the time, they do add their name. The great thing about this is I can now have a great conversation around their idea or feedback without trying to generalize.

However you do it, holding a safe space for your team will produce results you can achieve in no other way. Put the ego aside and hold that space for the team. You will be happy you did.

7 – Listen More than You Talk

Listening can be a powerful tool for a leader. While active listening is the basis for this, the other part, that is harder to accomplish, is to listen more than you speak. As leaders, we came up through the ranks, we saw and experienced much of what our teams are going through. We want to be helpful because we know what is going on. Or at least we think we do.

This is where listening to the situation and allowing your team to fill you in is critical. Our minds are already leaping ahead to a solution based on our experience. Be careful about what you think you know. We may not have the whole picture. There may be key differences from what we have seen previously. We need to listen and be aware of the feelings in the room. When we blaze ahead without sensing how what we are saying is landing, we can misstep.

I had just arrived at NOSC Alameda and was stepping into the CO role as my predecessor briefed me on the specifics of how things were working. My role at that point was to observe and get to know the staff in preparation for taking over. The current CO was a very successful officer. He had accomplished a great deal in his career and was going on to lead a team flying executive transport in Europe following this tour. I didn't really know him and was trying to get a feel for how things were running at the NOSC. I had just come from the Naval War College earning my master's degree and was fresh from the insights provided during my leadership studies.

At the NOSC there was a first-class petty officer who was an active-duty sailor. He did not report to the NOSC CO, instead, he reported to one of the assigned units. From what I gathered talking to the outgoing NOSC CO, this sailor was lacking in several areas. He called the sailor into his office and had him standing at attention in front of his desk while he proceeded to list his shortcomings and berate the sailor on how he should be performing versus how he was performing.

I was witness to this event, and I could see, being apart from the process, that the sailor's attitude was one of "I really don't care what you are saying, I don't work for you." I continued to observe the NOSC CO list the sailor's shortcomings and all I could think was that he had absolutely no idea how he was showing up. He was not listening to the mood of the room. He was not seeing that his efforts at dressing down this petty officer were having no impact whatsoever.

This event did color my opinion of the outgoing CO. I saw that he did not know how he was showing up to the team. This lesson was lost on him. I also took it as a lesson for myself to try and listen more and be more aware of the mood in the room.

This goes back to active listening and how are you showing up. Later, when I was the CO and made a similar misstep, interrupting my supply leading petty officer when I was intent on getting my point across, I was not listening to what she was saying. It was not on point to my question. At the same time, I made a snap judgement and did not hear what she was trying to tell me. Whether or not the information was what I needed, my team member was trying to meet my needs. As leaders we need to make the effort to meet the needs of our teams. If we listen more than we speak, we can understand the perspectives of our teams and how we can best support the overall effort.

Today, years later, with many more experiences such as these under my belt, I do my best to make it part of how I show up. I want to listen to the team; I want to listen to the person I am interacting with so I can understand their perspective before I engage the problem-solving part of my brain. I love to work the issue, to solve the problem, but if we charge ahead without fully understanding the issues, our efforts just may be in vain.

8 – Empathy is a Superpower

When I was in the Navy in San Diego, while taking a post-graduate distance learning course, I was introduced to the book *Emotional Intelligence* by Daniel Goleman. This book, unlike many books I have read for classes, had a significant impact on me. I learned about emotional intelligence as a concept; this was a new thing for me. I felt I was somewhat empathetic at that point in my life, yet I was learning an entirely new concept around how to be emotionally intelligent.

While studying the subject, I could see how, by being more emotionally intelligent, I would be able to empathize in a more open and centered way. Being able to regulate emotions, I believe, opens us up to being able to be more empathetic towards others. I highly recommend learning more about emotional intelligence. While Intelligence alone cannot be learned, emotional intelligence can, and there is power in it.

The point of this is that empathy is a large part of being a good leader. Being able to understand how another person is feeling in the moment allows a level of connection. This connection can build trust and support the efforts of a leader. It also allows the leader to better understand what may be happening in the lives of their team so they can support the people who they work with and for in a more substantial way. The reality is people feel what and how they feel. These feelings, even if we disagree, are real.

My first real experience with empathy in the workplace was while I was the chief of staff at Destroyer Squadron One. The Commodore and much of the staff were out on a short deployment and I was in charge back at home. One of the duties of the Commodore, or the person standing in for them, was to have a check out brief with departing department heads from the assigned ships.

One morning, I was scheduled to hold one of these conversations with an officer departing a ship. She came into the office and helped me remember she had been an enlisted sailor in one of my aviation squadrons. She had gone on to attain her commission as an officer and selected surface warfare.

I was a land-based aviator my entire career, I was just learning what life was like for the personnel assigned to the surface ship Navy. I was honestly amazed, based on my observations, that the surface Navy was able to retain people due to the challenges of life when assigned to a ship. Long hours, long at-sea periods even when at home, and long deployments.

This officer was up for promotion, and she was a stellar performer. She had excelled in her role on the ship, and we were having a good conversation about what her prospects were for the future. She then let me know about how disillusioned she was about her personal life. She let me know that she had no time for the things that many of us take for granted. She could not sustain a relationship, she wanted children, yet she did not see how this would be possible given the demands of the career she had chosen.

I listened and made every effort to empathize. I spoke very little and asked her what mattered most. I made no effort to offer a solution. This was not my issue; I was simply being present for her to express her frustration about the situation. I let her know I was there any time she wanted to discuss the possibilities for her future in the Navy or otherwise. She left my office happier, I think, than when she arrived. Being present and empathetic made a difference.

Many years later, in my current role, the team was bringing on a group of new analysts. We had never hired four at once and this was an exciting time. One of the new hires was very close to giving birth when we hired her, and our HR department wanted to know if we wanted to wait to bring her on until after she gave birth. We had made the decision to hire them all and wanted them to be part of the team as quickly as possible. We brought them all on board. Two weeks later, she went on maternity leave.

During her maternity leave, we discovered that another member of her family was severely ill. This illness had been treated previously but returned while she was on maternity leave. Even though the employee did not have enough time banked, we supported her and the family through an extended period. Why? Because we view our team as family. We support the entire team all the time. Empathy plays a major role in how we work with each other.

Working in a large team, we've experienced many situations like this. From an employee who was not meeting expectations, to those with family members having challenges with health or other issues. We approach each with empathy, we support the team members, and we support the larger team. Empathy is not just about supporting the teammate with the issue. Those issues can call people away from work and the work must be completed. This means the rest of the team must pick up the slack. Treating the entire team with empathy, overtly thanking them for their efforts, and being available to listen if they have questions or challenges with how things are going has been critical to the overall success of the team.

Empathy is not just being "touchy-feely.'" Empathy is about supporting your team so that together, the mission gets completed.

9 – Set Your Intention Each Day – And Meet It

Be How You Want to Be

Something I think is important that I've written about here already is the concept of how I want to show up each day. It is a recurring theme for me. Others may think about this in terms of "how I want to be." For me it is setting a daily intention in life and work. How do I want to be today? One of the ways I share this with my team is by saying, "If your intention is to be a jerk, and at the end of the day, you have been a jerk, well good for you!" The point is to show up as you intend each day. This goes for all aspects of life.

One morning shortly after taking charge of my team, I heard that one of the people who monitor for hazards had not been able to be reached. When he was finally contacted, he stated his phone had run out of charge and he wasn't able to charge it at that moment. This was an obvious evasion; we have a multitude of tools for remaining in communication when we are working. This was the first not ok situation with my team, and I wanted to make a point.

I summoned the entire team into a call and read them the riot act about keeping their phones charged and being available the entire time they were on duty. I likened not being available to falling asleep on watch while in the military. Absolutely unacceptable. The team heard me loud and clear, or I thought they had.

I was later contacted by one of my team members who asked what that was all about. I realized that even though I and the leaders who work for me along several other team members knew what had happened, some did not or were not aware of the situation. I showed up apparently angry and some of the team had no idea why. This was not my intention on how to show up for the team and I realized I had an opportunity to get better.

At the next all hands call I explained the situation for the team and let them know that I had failed to ensure the entire team was aware of what happened. That was my bad and I apologized and promised to ensure all were informed in the future. For me it was a great lesson to slow down when I had a message to communicate and ensure I was showing up as I intended.

Setting a daily intention is a mindful practice. It takes effort and thought. At the same time, don't overthink the idea. Ask yourself what you want to accomplish and how you want to show up. Once you have the basics in mind on how you want to be for your team it's time to observe whether or not you have succeeded.

For this part, set a short amount of time aside at the end of the workday. Ask yourself how you met your intention that day. Were you successful?

The other part of this is something I do with my team on a regular basis. I have one-on-one calls with my direct reports every two weeks. I make these sacrosanct unless one of us is out of the office. I may need to adjust the time, yet I ensure that each day they are scheduled, they occur. At the end of the check-in, I always try to ask the same question, What I have I screwed up for you lately? This is me being real with my team. I want to know if I have done anything to mess up their work. I also want to know if I have made their work more challenging through what I have done. Most of the time I am told there is nothing to report. While I appreciate the positive feedback, I cannot improve how I show up without honest feedback. It's nice, yet nothing constructive comes from it. Whenever I am told there was something I should look at, I get very interested and even excited.

For me, this kind of constructive feedback is what I refer to as my gold nuggets. This type of open and honest feedback is one of the biggest gifts my team can provide. This is because I can use that to examine how I have been showing up and adjust to get better. This is how I learn from the team about whether I'm meeting my intentions.

10 – Have a Plan (Vision)

In the introduction to this book, I made a statement that leadership is a choice. Some people who are placed in leadership positions are not up to the task. Making the choice to be a leader and succeed in the role means moving the needle with the team. This means the leader must move the team in the direction required for success. To achieve success, the team must have a plan and a vision to see what the future state can be. Some of the measures of success will be given by others, some will be developed within the team. As the leader, you must have that plan and vision as your north star. You oversee the direction the team will move, and that requires a plan.

During my last squadron tour, I was contacted by my detailer--the person who sends officers to their next assignment--and told I would be heading to NOSC Tulsa the following summer. I was excited and called the current CO and let him know I had just received verbal orders to be his replacement. I felt his response was odd as he said,

"That's weird, I thought I was staying until February." I didn't think much of this at the time as I had work to do.

A few months later, I received my written orders to NOSC Tulsa. I again called the current CO and let him know I had received my written orders and would be arriving in August as his relief. To my dismay, his response, again, was "That's weird, I thought I wasn't leaving until February." This set off alarm bells in my mind. Here was an officer, in charge of 250 Navy reserve personnel, who gave the identical response, months apart, when told he was being relieved early. This officer did not, in either instance, call his detailer, or his boss, and ask what was going on. This lack of curiosity and concern about what was happening led me to believe I was going to inherit a mess.

When I arrived at NOSC Tulsa, that CO was nowhere to be found. He realized he was being relieved early and worked with his detailer and received orders to depart within a couple of months. I later discovered he had been very close to being fired for lack of confidence in his ability to command. I was ordered in early to take over and notionally make things better at the center.

I came in and took stock of what was going on, and realized the team was in desperate need of leadership. I have shared some of how I showed up already, and I kept that going. I was there for the reservists and to ensure their families were supported. I quickly put in place the processes I was familiar with and worked to support these patriots as they continued their service along with their civilian work.

One of the ways I wanted to ensure support for the reservists was to be the visible face of the Navy for their families. Towards the end of my time at the NOSC, a large unit was being mobilized to head over to Iraq. This can be extremely stressful for the reservists and their families. Adding to the stress was the deployment date was December 26th. I knew I needed to be visible and available to the families while their reserve sailors were on active duty in the war zone. I already had a great ombudsman at the center who was the point of contact for all families. The Navy ombudsman program is excellent, and I gave all the support I could to ensure this connection was active.

The other thing I did to show the deploying team support and let the families know I was there for them was to show up at the place and time of their departure. The day after Christmas, I got up early and showed up at the airport in my uniform at 4am. The entire unit was there, and I was there as a visible symbol of the thing that was taking their loved ones away. My intention that morning was to have the families direct their ire and anger at the deployment toward me and not their loved ones. It was an uncomfortable morning, and it was more than worth it.

Taking the NOSC from a failing center, to one of the top performing centers in the region in 23 months was my goal. By supporting my team and with their support, I achieved that goal. I did this through using the tools I had learned over my career. I made mistakes, and I still saw success. After I departed the center for my next assignment, I was elated to learn every one of those sailors returned home from that deployment alive.

In 2020 I started the role I am in while I write this. I could see right away that I had joined a high-performing team. This was a team of true professionals who were and remain passionate about the work we do. I also saw there were some things that needed attention:

- There were little to no documented processes for the team. They were operating mostly through tribal knowledge.
- There was very little career progression available to the team.
- The team was operating with far fewer people than were needed for the task at hand.

Very soon after I arrived, I shared my vision for the future of the team. We worked together to put in place formal processes and procedures. We worked with internal and external stakeholders to improve how we operated and ensure total support. I was able to communicate the need for career progression and was able to put in place a level for employees to take on additional duties and receive promotions. We were also able to make the case to expand the team to the numbers required to do the work being asked.

The team has remained a high-functioning one throughout. We built the vision collaboratively. I was able to share the vision I had with them and we continue to improve the processes and future for the team.

Through sharing my plan and vision, by including the team in that work and allowing them to add to the plan, I have been able to build buy-in for the future. We have worked together on the vision and each of them are co-owners. I have every confidence the team will continue to move the work forward after I depart. I have set the team up to succeed each other and, eventually move into my role as they continue to perform the work. The team needs to be able to see the career progression and how they can move along that progression. This builds in succession and ensures future leaders will come from within the team.

11 – Develop the Leaders of the Future

For me, one of the greatest roles for a leader is to develop the leaders who will come after. Those future leaders will carry on the work we all do and keep the teams running smoothly and well through the years ahead.

In my last Navy tour as the CO of NOSC Alameda, I had the opportunity to work with my first executive officer (XO) on several things to ensure his success and support to the Navy.

One of the things that needs to occur to view the potential of an officer is to review their performance record. I asked the XO to bring me his record so I could review where I thought he should focus. I was stunned to see that on his final tour aboard a ship, he was given a fitness report--equivalent to a performance appraisal--that did not make any sense. His performance for me had been stellar and he was a thoughtful and reasonable officer. As I read the fitness report from this ship CO, I saw there were several issues.

The Navy fitness reporting system as I knew it had many shortfalls. One of these was forced ranking, meaning only a certain percentage of the officers being rated could be rated highly. The other was the numerical grading system. Each CO had an average number for the level of officer they wrote fitness reports on. If your report was at or above this average number, it was seen as positive, below negative. Fitness reports were typically performed annually, unless the reporting senior departed, then they were performed upon that person's departure, or if the officer departed, in which case they were not ranked against their peers.

This is what is known as a one of one report. If there were no comparators, then the report was just the officer with no competition. Competitive reports were desired as they showed how the officer performed against their peers during the time. The five possible ratings are:

- Significant Problems
- Progressing
- Promotable
- Must Promote
- Early Promote

Typically, when an officer was departing a command, they were given a one of one with a recommendation of early promote. This is the top rating the CO can give, and when there is no competition and no reason to reduce the rating. It is normal to be rated this way in this circumstance.

When I reviewed my XO's last fitness report from the ship, I saw he was one of one, with a promotable rating. This was what was known as a 'double airgap', meaning the CO could have rated the officer more highly, and chose not to. Not only that, but he also chose to rate this officer two marks below where he could have. I was stunned. The report also showed a decline in the numerical rating from the previous report. Normally, a promotion board will look for a reason in the write-up on the report indicating why these actions were taken. In this case, there was nothing in the write-up to explain the declining report. The report as written was a potential career ending issue for my XO. This was not representative of the officer who was working for me.

I knew I had to do something to remedy this situation. My XO was a stellar officer and did not deserve what this report would do to his career. One of the other issues the Navy has is many junior officers are unaware of how to view their fitness reports. They have no experience on promotion boards, and no one has taken the time to explain the process and thinking behind it to them.

I did the only thing I could think of, I called the senior officer in our community to ask his advice. The Full-time support community is specialized in the management of reserve members of the Navy, and we had one admiral in the community. Most of us had a relationship with the admiral, and my XO knew him as well. I called him and explained the situation. I was at a loss at what to do. The admiral made a very smart recommendation. He simply said, "Call the guy, and ask." This made a lot of sense to me, so that's what I did.

I called the captain, who at that time was assigned to the Pentagon, and explained what I was seeing, and how the XO was performing. I explained these two things did not match at all and I was wondering how we might be able to remedy the situation. The captain understood and explained it had been a stressful time aboard the ship. The previous CO had been relieved for cause, and he was just "cleaning house." He agreed to write a letter of support for my XO.

The letter arrived and basically stated that the fitness report he had written was not indicative of the value of this officer and he was obviously succeeding. This was addressed to any promotion or selection board and essentially invalidated the negative report.

The first indication we had that we were successful was when my XO was selected to be the CO of a smaller reserve center a few months later. This was a great and positive sign. Shortly after I retired from the Navy, the promotion board results were released for advancement to lieutenant commander. I knew the XO was being considered, and when I saw his name on the selection list, I knew we had succeeded in fixing the issue. The elation I felt when I saw his name on that list was better than when I had seen my own name on similar lists in the past. I felt vindicated.

I spent a lot of time developing my XO into a solid and effective leader. I wanted to ensure he could succeed if he wanted to remain in the Navy. I am pleased to say he is still in the Navy today; at the same rank I was when I retired. I still speak with him on occasion, and he is at the same crossroads I was when I decided to leave. The fact that he can make that choice, and it is not being made for him speaks to the success of our efforts all those years ago.

Today, I have six leaders who report to me. Each of them are people leaders who have a variety of strengths and opportunities. None of them are the same. None of them are even terribly similar. They all have different areas where I can see opportunities for personal growth. As their leader, I see it as a large part of my job to help them develop.

One of these leaders is exceptionally competent from a technical perspective. His ability to get to the heart of the matter and ensure the reporting is done to a high level of competence has been superb. He is a true get the job done kind of person.

The other side of the coin has been his development in the emotional intelligence realm. Since the day I walked in as the new leader of the team, I saw the opportunities for him to excel not just in the realm of technical expertise, but also in the realm of being a people leader who shows he cares and can listen and develop his people in a manner that will be effective into the future.

Over the past five years we have worked on that. I have coached him to look at how he is showing up and how he wants to show up. I have encouraged him to see how he might achieve more satisfying results if he adjusted his approach slightly to show more of the personal side.

I am very pleased to report that the work has been successful. This leader now shows up in a new manner. Not radically different from before. Just a little more approachable. He thinks about challenges in a slightly different way. He is a more well-rounded person and is achieving more effective end results.

This is the work that we do as leaders. We collaborate with our teams, and we work on their flat spots to help round them out and work to achieve better results.

One of the things that truly bothers me as a leader is when I receive two-week's notice from a team member that they have found a new role. Two weeks is seen, in general, as the minimum appropriate amount of time to give notice. While I understand that, there is a large piece missing when this occurs.

I make it clear to my team that if they are seeking another role, we can and should talk about it. I fully support the desires of anyone on my team to pursue other roles inside or outside the company. Here's the thing, I know people. I can help. We can have a great conversation around the thinking about why they are looking to move. Most of the time it is about advancement opportunities. My team is very high functioning, and there are few opportunities to move up. They do happen, yet I completely understand if someone does not want to wait for the next spot to open. This is part of life and completely normal. I also am aware that others in the company sometimes seek to poach from my team as they know they will receive a solid employee. I see this is a high form of praise for what we are doing.

My point around this is to have the discussion. Let's talk about why the move is being considered and about what opportunities may be coming on the team. I also want to be a sounding board for my team members who are considering moving so we can have an open and honest conversation around the reasoning. I try very hard to be balanced in these conversations and ensure the teammate is thinking it through before they apply to move on.

Most of the time they do and most of the time they are selected. I absolutely love this. It's great when someone on my team moves to a higher position. It speaks well for them and for the team. We develop our people to the point they are desired by other leaders. This also creates opportunity in my own team. If a supervisor who reports to me departs for another role, then I can provide an opportunity for someone on my team to move up. Career progression is also important to the development of our people.

Once a year my leaders and I look at the entire team for potential promotions. I have one demand of the leaders. Those they are recommending must have shown sustained superior performance.

Without that, the conversation ends quickly. New people are generally not considered as they have not had the opportunity to prove sustained performance. Those who are not showing leadership qualities or have been passed over and show their disappointment through a reduction in their work quality are those who still require additional coaching and development before we give them the shot. I expect a great deal from my people, but I think that if you asked any one of them if I am fair, they would say yes.

In the five years I have been in this role, we have had two self-select out and one termination. I am 100% ok with self-selecting out. We cannot and should not be forcing people into roles they do not want. Termination is a tough one. I always assume positive intent and we worked with this person for over two years to get his performance to a place where we could accept it. Sadly, we never got there. So, we had to remove him from the team. I always see this as the option of last resort. It is the single most unpleasant task for a leader. At the same time, when we get to that point, it is the best thing for the good of the team.

Having a solid process to review the team is crucial. Developing the leaders who report to you is critical. They are the ones who will be developing their people into their replacements just as I am developing my people to replace me. I feel very fortunate that I will not be the one making the decision when I depart. I know that any one of the leaders who report to me today could succeed in my role tomorrow. The fact that I have worked hard to develop them into my successors is how I know this. They will make it very challenging for my own leadership to choose. That's the point.

12 – Leadership is not Just Down – Manage Up – Without Fear

I have seen many leaders over the years who do not manage up. Managing up is, in my experience, sometimes even more important than managing down. Your boss's boss can crush the team just as brutally as anyone. Managing up and ensuring your own leadership is aware of how they are showing up is key to overall success for the team and the organization.

Managing up can be hazardous. There is no doubt about this truth. If your leader is not open to feedback and they do not make it safe to provide the feedback, there can be real risk to your position. This is where the operating without fear tenet comes in strong. If you are doing the right thing, and you can provide the feedback to your own leadership, then you will be better for it. If they choose not to integrate the feedback or if they choose not to accept it, that is not on you.

In the example I used about my second role at the company, where I provided strong feedback to my leader, he appreciated the feedback I gave. His behavior did change. He did not tell the team we were aligned on a subject without checking with me again. The leader in question was sometimes challenging to work under. He was very sure of how things should run and to make changes to that opinion, those of us working for him had to strongly make our case. There is nothing wrong with that situation, however it removes the assumption of trust in your team.

In the tenet of never operating from a position of fear, look back over the examples. Most of that was not only operating without fear, but it was also managing up. If you must stand up for your team and have a solid case to make, then you are managing the expectations of those you report to. I noticed an interesting change of behavior after letting the COO of the company know he already had people to do the task I was being asked to do with my team. For the remainder of that year, whenever the COO called me after hours, he apologized for calling late. I made it clear that it was ok, we do manage emergency situations and after hours is always fair game. I just noticed it was a change in behavior and a recognition of how he had been showing up.

In my current role I have several peers who are technically senior to me. I also report to a leader with whom I am more extremely aligned than any in my past. In this role I do whatever I can to coach my peers when they ask. They see me as being successful in navigating the company structure. My leader is at least as well read about these things as I am, often more so. Being recognized as a leader who is also a coach is, and should be, a humbling experience. For me it is also very rewarding.

As you learn who you want to be and how you want to show up. Think about how you will share the lessons you learned along the way. Up is always an option.

13 – Meet People Where They are, Not Where You Want Them to be

This can be a tough one to swallow. We want our teams to be as mature and effective as possible. We want the leaders we interact with to be as good or better than we are. We want our teams to instantly understand what we are talking about when we convey an idea. We want them to be on the same page as we are all the time.

This is not reality. Different people are just that, different. We are all at different stages in our own development. We have all done different work. We are seeking different things. We are hopefully moving in the same direction as a team. When we interact with our teammates, with those we support, with stakeholders, with anyone really; we must meet them where they are.

We cannot force others to be at our level. There is no magic to personal work. It takes time and effort. Some people are unwilling to put in that time and effort. Some people are going to be far beyond where we are in our own personal development. Our role is to make sure we are meeting them where they are. In the case of them being further along than we are, we need to have the courage to ask them to meet us where we are.

When I was a flight instructor in the Navy, I was an experienced aviator with several years of operational experience behind me. I knew what I was doing and how to make the aircraft do what I needed it to do. My students were intermediate or advanced flight students who had some experience. They were getting into the T-2C Buckeye jet trainer with anywhere from 110 to 250 flight hours of experience under their belt. I was back from a three-and-a-half-year fleet tour in addition to my own training background, including the instructor training syllabus for the aircraft. I was meeting them with somewhere between 1500 and 2000 flight hours of experience. I knew I had to instill in these students the confidence to fly the aircraft well and pass along any advice and techniques for them to be able to succeed.

One of the most challenging aspects of flying in Naval aviation is the carrier landing. It is an exercise in precision. I had not been a carrier aviator in the fleet as I had flown land-based patrol aircraft. The senior instructors had taught me the skills I needed to get the students to where they needed to be. One of the techniques I used was talking through the landing pattern for the student as I was demonstrating. I did not stop making comments on my own performance over the intercom through the entire pattern. Whatever I saw, whether I was on airspeed, altitude or glidepath or off, I vocalized the situation so the student could match what they were seeing with the corrections I was making. Being on airspeed, and on altitude and on glidepath in an aircraft is a momentary situation, we are always correcting, feeling the motion and adjusting to keep us as close as possible to that perfect state.

I was meeting the students where they were in their experience and had come up with a way to pass along what was going through my own head in each moment so they could learn. They were able to learn from my mistakes as well as my successes.

Years later, after I had stopped flying and was in San Francisco for Fleet Week, I was at a reception for the Blue Angels. I had recently promoted to commander and was mingling with the crowd at the event. One of the Blue Angels walked up to me and said, "Commander Ridgway, you were my flight instructor!" In that moment, I knew that young Marine had surpassed his teacher and then some. I was very proud to have been able to contribute to his success in some small way.

Today I have six leaders reporting to me. Each of them is in a different place in their own leadership development path. I schedule one-on-one meetings with each of them every two weeks. These are opportunities to check in, help resolve issues and provide feedback both to and from them. Each time I meet with them, and my other direct reports who do not manage other people, I meet them where they are. I listen and provide advice or encouragement. I cannot move them along their path at a pace faster than their own. I can only reinforce what we have talked about previously and how I think they might be able to progress.

Meeting each of my teammates where they are is extremely satisfying. Over time I can see their progress and gauge how to encourage them into the next phase of their own personal and professional development.

14 – Own Your Successes and Your Fails

Ownership is critical to the success of your team. However they perform, you must own that. Whenever one of your team members messes up, you must own that. Whenever one of them has success, you must celebrate that. When one of your team has the next great idea, you must credit them with that. You, as the leader, will get more credit than is your due simply by creating the culture in which they can thrive and do their work.

Owning your failures and sharing them can be just as powerful as successes. In my roles both in the Navy and after, safety is a large part of what we do. One of the things I began doing as the CO of NOSC Tulsa and continue to do to this day is share personal safety stories. I have many stories of how I failed to follow safety protocols and either did, or nearly, hurt myself. I have the scars to prove it. When you share times when you failed with your team, you show vulnerability. The armor of the leader has chinks and pointing them out to your team proves to them that you are a fallible human just as they are. At this point I have a lengthy list of personal safety mess-ups, and I share them with the team whenever there is an ask for a safety story. Personal stories are more impactful and help convey the message more strongly than slogans or trite sayings. We can put passion into our personal stories that simply does not exist when we are conveying a message from another source.

The same goes for success. When anyone on the team has success, it is a reason to celebrate. Recognizing the effort and the impact of the work can have far-reaching effects. Bragging about how well your team is doing to your own leadership, holding up a teammate as an example for others, showing the team the impact of their work on the overall success of the organization. All of these are valuable.

I have been fortunate to have a great deal of success in the work I am doing. The team I am leading has a purpose to help keep the public, our customers and coworkers safe. The team is comprised of amazing and dedicated professionals. My own leadership sees their value and recognizes that frequently. This role has been the most rewarding of my career.

Contrast that to my previous role. I enjoyed the work, I enjoyed the team. We were also focused on keeping people safe. The team of aviators I was leading were and are excellent. On the other hand, another part of my team was the most challenging I ever led. When I look back on how I showed up for that part of the team, I can see where I failed. It was a daily effort on my part to keep the group working together. I set myself up for failure when I came into that role. I was trying to be everyone's friend. I was trying to push teammates with very different approaches to work together and just get the job done. I was not meeting the team where they were, I was trying to force them to be where I wanted them to be.

For me this turned into daily work to keep them functioning. I spent far too much time playing the peacekeeper for that part of the team. I saw success in keeping them functioning, yet as I look back on that, I can see that it was not sustainable.

One day, in the first week of March of 2020, my position was eliminated. That meant that it was my last day in that role, and I needed to seek out a new role within the company. My immediate concern was for the team and how they would continue to function without me being there. I knew that without my daily interactions with the part of the team that was not working well together, they would absolutely fall apart. I made myself indispensable to that part of the team, yet my leadership was unaware of what I was doing.

The result was as I expected. The portion of the team I was working so hard to keep going, fell apart. They failed spectacularly and it was, at least partly, my fault. Maybe more than partly. Within a few months they had all been let go and replaced with on-call contract workers. That small part of the larger team was and remains my most challenging personnel issue ever.

It would be easy for me to blame the leader who decided to eliminate my position. It would be easy for me to blame the team members who were failing to work well together. It would be easy for me to blame my own leader for not seeing the potential impact of his leader's decision on the team.

The reality is this was my issue to own. We will not always succeed in our efforts. If we keep trying the same thing over and over expecting a different result, well, we all know what that is the definition of.

The result of my being pushed out of that role became what I consider the best opportunity of my professional career. I was forced out of my comfort zone. Just over two months later, and during the

COVID-19 pandemic, I was given the opportunity to lead the team and do the work that has become so fulfilling.

We can never know what the future holds. We can only do our best in the space we are provided. While I thought I was doing my best in my previous role, in hindsight, I can see I was stuck in a rut. Being forced out of that rut has allowed me to continue the journey of leadership and apply everything I learned to a different team with a great deal more success than I ever dreamed possible.

15 – Summarizing the Advanced Tenets of Leadership

I still feel the largest obstacle to success for most people is fear. I have experienced this, and seen others operate from that position. Leaving it behind and moving forward in a respectful and professional manner has proved to be one of the greatest leaps forward. Fear has its place, allowing it to control you is not that place.

As we lead those who are or will become leaders, we owe them the right to learn and lead. We must allow them to practice what they have learned and find their perspective and manner of leadership. We are not clones of each other and should not be. As unique individuals, we will find the things that speak to us and allow us to be the best leaders we can be. Backing up those who lead for us or will lead in the future goes a long way to showing them they can be successful in the role.

As we journey down this road of leading others in a common purpose, we must continue to learn. Learning from those around us, those we work for, those who have come before, and those who will follow us is crucial to the success of the team. Expanding our knowledge through experience, formal learning, and self-assessment can be powerful and game changing. Doing the work to learn who we are at our core and what speaks to us is essential.

Not all leaders are good at leading. We will see and experience a variety of leadership examples as we travel this road. The thing is, even the ones we view as poor leaders have something to teach us. We can often learn more from them than we do from the ones we appreciate.

Failure is an option. At least in the moment. We should be holding a safe space for those we lead to try new ideas and learn from them. If the ideas succeed, that's awesome. If they fail, what can we learn from the failed attempt? Creating a safe culture to fail forward produces breakthrough results.

We need to know what our teammates are thinking and how they are feeling about the work. They may not express that if they don't feel like it's safe to do so. Holding a safe space for the expression of ideas and opinions, and proving that safety through repetition, can bring out the best in our people. We want them to speak up when they have a question or something to say. Be inquisitive and show them you are interested in their opinions and questions. Participate in the dialogue and see where it leads.

If we push our thoughts out without pausing to listen, we run the risk of shutting down our team in their expression of their own ideas and thoughts. Listening can be difficult, especially when there are critical events and operations going on. Taking the time to listen more than we talk allows our team members to express what's on their minds. Who knows, that next great idea from your team may change the whole game.

Empathy and emotional intelligence fold directly into these tenets. Being able to allow your team to express their emotions and keeping it safe and supportive empowers your team to thrive. We all have reality crashing down on us from time to time. Being there for the team, making it more like a work family, and meaning it, speaks volumes for the satisfaction your team has on the job.

What was your intention today? Did you meet that intention? Are you showing up how you meant to? Ask yourself these questions in the moment, at the end of the day, whenever it makes sense. Receiving the feedback from yourself, from those you work with and those you partner with is a gift. Treat it as such.

When we move into a team, we need to observe, listen, ask questions, and then work out what the next steps are going to be. Implementing the tenets and learning what the team needs will inform the plans that move them into the future. As the leader, they will look to you for that plan, at least initially. As the plan forms, and is executed, the team needs to be able to influence the nuances of the plan so they can be owners of the outcome.

The members of the teams we lead have their own strengths and opportunities for growth. Getting to know each of them and helping them develop into the future leaders they will become is both challenging and rewarding. This is a joint effort between your teammates and you as the leader. Developing future leaders ensures your successors will be ready when it's time for you to move on.

Have the courage to manage up as well as down. Help develop your peers and leaders. Give them the professional and honest feedback they need to achieve success. This can be tough and may not be safe depending on the leader. Can we continue to work with and for leaders who do not accept feedback? It makes success difficult.

It can be challenging to meet people where they are. We so want them to be where we want them to be. We must learn to recognize how we can help our teams level up and become more. It takes time, patience, and support. Showing up as the leader we want to be, this is how we can succeed.

Vulnerability is challenging for most people. Being vulnerable was my breakthrough in the deep personal development course my first boss outside the Navy sent me through. It's easy to tout our successes and victories. Being able to own our failures is the work. Sharing the lessons learned and showing others that we are there to give them the credit for the win and not going to blame them for the fails goes a long way to building interdependence in your team.

THE WRAP-UP

Leadership is a choice. Some people are in positions of leadership and are not leaders. We must choose to lead. The title is just that, words. The job is so much more. Being a leader comes with so much weight. Responsibility for your team, for your team's results, for your own results. This can weigh us down until we feel like we can no longer move.

Moving past the weight, choosing to be the leader we know we can be. Admitting when we don't know the best answer and are working on it. Being vulnerable with our teams, coworkers, leaders and selves can be a massive challenge. Ego tells us not to admit our shortcomings.

How we show up each day to our team, to our coworkers, to our leadership. This is what matters. Have we built a culture of transparency and trust? Are we taking care of our people? Are we meeting our intentions each and every day? These are the things that enable success.

This book is my attempt to pass along many of the tenets I have learned as a leader through more than three decades of being in a leadership position. From my 23 years in the Navy and all the personal and professional challenges I found in that career. To the 11 plus years in my current company as a member of several different teams across a large organization. I have learned, as best I can, who I am as a leader.

The basic tenets shared here are the foundation on which to build more. Without the foundation, the building cannot stand. Without the middle, the top cannot be supported. Leaders are made, not born. Charisma can get you only so far in life. As we continue to move onward and upward, we must continue to learn and apply the lessons to become more.

Do I have all the answers? I certainly hope not. I am not any sort of leadership messiah. I am not a guru. I am someone who was thrown into leadership in my mid-20s and has been in that space ever since. In some cases, I was supported and taught, in others I was thrown into the deep end to see if I could swim. Having been through all of that, and feeling like I might have something to share, has led me to this endeavor.

I truly hope you are inspired by some of these stories. I know I take a great deal of satisfaction in putting into words what has been rattling around in my brain for many years. But this isn't everything.

We are all just beginning.

RECOMMENDED READING LIST

I mentioned a variety of other books here that I've found helpful in my leadership journey. They are listed below here by title and author as recommended reading. Your mileage may vary, but I use what I've learned from them nearly every day.

It's Your Ship: Management Techniques from the Best Damn Ship in the Navy by Michael Abrashoff

Lincoln On Leadership: Executive Strategies for Tough Times by Donald T. Phillips

Emotional Intelligence by Daniel Goleman

The Dichotomy of Leadership: Balancing the Challenges of Extreme Ownership to Lead and Win by Jocko Willink and Leif Babin

Extreme Ownership: How U.S. Navy SEALs Lead and Win by Jocko Willink and Leif Babin

GLOSSARY AND EXPLANATION

My wife, Sarah, brought up a great point while she was helping me edit this book. Not everyone understands some of the terms I use. There are several Navy terms and other items that would benefit from a little advanced preparation for the reader who may not be familiar. I will still try to explain in the text, but, here is a short glossary of terms for reference.

AOCS – Aviation Officer's Candidate School. This was my accession source into the Navy. It was a sixteen-week program when I went through. The main training is provided by Marine Corps drill instructors. If you have watched *An Officer and a Gentleman,* you will get the idea.

Gunny – a common reference to a Marine Corps Gunnery Seargent. My drill instructor was a Gunnery Seargent at the time I knew him. The common reference to this rank is "Gunny".

CO – Commanding Officer. This is the officer in overall command of a Navy/Military unit. This person is responsible for the good order and discipline for that unit and sometimes subordinate units.

XO – Executive Officer. When assigned, this is the second-in-command of the unit. This officer reports to the CO. They can give orders and run things when the CO is away. Think of them as a CO in training.

P-3 Orion or P-3C - This was the main aircraft I flew while in the Navy. I started out as a 'No-P' or unqualified pilot and worked my way up over 18 months to become a Patrol Plane Commander, responsible for the safe operation of the aircraft and her crew. The P-3C is/was a maritime patrol and submarine hunting aircraft. It is a large, land-based aircraft. The P-3 first came into service in the 1960s and continues to fly today with a variety of militaries. The US P-3C aircraft has a crew of 11 or 12 people, depending on the timeline and mission.

Ailerons - These are the flight control surfaces on an aircraft that allow it to turn. They are on the trailing edges of the wings and change the airflow to make the aircraft bank left or right and thus turn in that direction.

Navy Operational Support Center (NOSC) - These facilities used to be called Navy Reserve Centers. In the early 2000s they were changed to Navy Operational Support Centers. Typically, the Navy CO is in charge of the facility and there is a United States Marine Corps reserve unit assigned. In some cases there may be other services based at the facility. Recently the Navy has changed NOSCs back to Navy Reserve Centers.

Leader Standard Work - This is a Lean concept in business. In a basic sense this is the daily/weekly/monthly work that must be completed by the leader to perform their role.

Lean – There is much content out in the world about Lean concepts and how they help to make our daily work more efficient. I will not be explaining Lean here.

Command And Control Culture – This concept is descriptive of a culture where those at the top give orders and control the decisions of the organization. Feedback is not typically given or even desired. This is very typical of a military organization where orders are expected to be followed.

Navy Reservist - Reserve officers and enlisted members are part-time Navy personnel. They typically travel to their Navy work site, also known as a drill site, one weekend per month and work Saturday and Sunday. Each day has two drill periods which the reservists are paid for. There are also usually additional drills available for some reservists to perform extra work during the year. Each reservist is also expected to spend two weeks per year, minimum, on active duty.

Senior Enlisted Leader (SEL) - The Senior Enlisted Leader is the senior enlisted member assigned to a command. This role, much like the XO, is there to support the CO in their daily work. At the same time, the SEL is meant to be the voice of the enlisted personnel to the command. In some commands, the SEL is essentially the Executive Officer as there is no XO assigned. In the absence of the CO, the SEL would make command decisions. COs are wise to take the advice of their SEL seriously.

Navy Ombudsman Program – This program is designed to support the families of service members, especially when those service members are sent away from home for long periods of time. The ombudsman is typically the spouse of one of the personnel assigned to the unit and trained by the Navy about the program and resources available to support families when needed. The ombudsman will ideally work hand-in-hand with the leadership of the command to ensure awareness of difficulties being faced by the families. In this way, the command can work to provide support that may be needed by the family while allowing the service member to continue to perform their critical duties while away from home.

Navy Reserve Squadron OIC - When the CO and XO of a Navy reserve squadron are reservists, there is a need for an active-duty officer to be present and in charge when they are not on site. This is the Officer in Charge or OIC. This officer acts in their stead during the majority of the time as the reserve CO and XO are not expected to be at the squadron except on drill weekends and during their two-week active-duty time each year. This program was ended in 2010 when the Navy chose to alternate the CO and XO between active-duty and reserve officers. The XO becomes the new CO when the old CO departs.

Captain's Mast - This is a Navy term relating to non-judicial punishment. The Commanding Officer is empowered to mete out punishment for violations of the Uniform Code of Military Justice

(UCMJ) that do not rise to the level of requiring a legal procedure with attorneys and a judge.

Fitness Report – Officers in the military are given fitness reports on an annual basis, similar to a performance appraisal in the civilian world. There are other times when they will also receive fitness reports. These include when their reporting senior officer departs and when they depart the command they are assigned to. Officer fitness reports are an evaluation of the traits, strengths, and opportunities the officer exhibits. There are two main sections. First, there is a numerical grade that is an average of several important qualities. Then there is a writeup that should support the numerical grade.

A note on the relationship between a reserve center Commanding Officer (CO) and the Commanding Officers of the reserve units assigned to the center:

Navy Operational Support Centers (NOSCs) (now Navy Reserve Centers) are commanded by officers from the grade of Lieutenant through Captain. The grades are numbered – O-3 to O-6 (officer grade 3 to officer grade 6 – in the other services, captain through colonel) depending on the size of the NOSC. The CO of the NOSC has administrative responsibility for many of the requirements for the assigned reserve units. It can be challenging for a NOSC CO who is a lieutenant (O-3) to tell a unit CO who is a captain (O-6) what to do. This sets the typical junior/senior relationship on its head. It is important for the NOSC CO to have the ability to navigate that relationship of respect for the officer and their rank and balance it with the need to ensure the unit is meeting the needs of the Navy.

A word about Navy promotions and Selection boards:

Naval personnel are selected for promotion based on their performance over time. Generally, the higher the rank, the more challenging it is to be selected for promotion or that next big job. The rank of Lieutenant Commander in the Navy is typical for a department head role in a squadron for an aviation officer. The big jobs in the squadron are the operations officer and the maintenance officer. These two roles are (or were) seen as the most important for career development for an aviation officer. Without at least one of those roles under their belt, an aviation officer department head will be less likely to be selected for promotion to full Commander. The other challenge for officers is the competitive nature of the fitness reporting cycle. The

Navy evaluates their officers one time per year. At that time the officers are rated against others at the same rank within the same unit. The general rule again is those at the top of the pile have the best chances for promotion or selection. It is also important to be in a group of officers at the same rank so the report is seen as competitive. Outperforming your peers is the best way to stand out from the crowd.

ACKNOWLEDGEMENTS

I truly want to thank my wife, Sarah, for reading all the versions of this book and keeping me honest through the process. It has been quite a journey and what you have just finished is far better than what I first presented to her.

Joe Rafter was my first boss and the man who hired me into the utility company straight out of the Navy. He was willing to wait nearly six months while I finished my Navy career and transitioned to the civilian world. His trust, leadership, and guidance in the early part of my civilian career enabled me to become who I am today. I am truly honored that he agreed to write the foreword to this book. He remains a great friend to this day.

I first met Robin Braun while I was assigned to VP-92 in Brunswick, Maine. She was reviewing the safety programs of a sister squadron and tapped me to help with the process. She went on to lead the entire Navy Reserve and retire as a vice admiral. I reconnected with her as I was finishing this book, and she very graciously agreed to read it and provide feedback. She also helped me remember some details I had forgotten about the Navy fitness reporting system and filled in some knowledge gaps around how the Navy Reserve has changed since I retired. She is a strong leader and was an exceedingly effective chief of the Naval Reserve.

Creighton Ho was my XO at NOSC Alameda. He is currently still serving in the Navy and has continued to be a great officer in the years since we served together. I value his continued friendship and love that he agreed to provide a short review of this book.

Angie Gibson is my boss. She is a phenomenal leader who leads with her head, heart and hands. She has done the work and continues to inspire me every day. Sooner than she wants, I will be retiring for good, and I truly appreciate her guidance and feedback on this book.

Last but not least, the team at Zolly House – Lyle and Heather Smith. This dynamic duo has been the glue that held this project together. I went to high school with Lyle, and we reconnected during the Pandemic. We created "Pandemic Date Night" and held video calls every week for over 18 months without a miss! We have watched their son grow into an amazing young man and are very honored to call them friends. When they started Zolly House, I knew I had to get off my butt and really get this book done. Their feedback and edits have made this book so much better.

We all learn every day – keep doing it and being the best you can.

ABOUT THE AUTHOR

Jim Ridgway grew up in the rolling hills and jughandle roads of Bernardsville, New Jersey before heading to Albright College for a degree in Business. Somewhere along the way, the call of the open skies — and a good challenge — lured him to Aviation Officer's Candidate School, launching a 23-year career as a U.S. Naval aviator and leader.

Navy adventures took him around the world and then some. Deployment to the Middle East, Southeast Asia and the Eastern Pacific. He also served as Commanding Officer of not one, but two Navy Operational Support Centers, and as the Chief of Staff for Destroyer Squadron One. He also earned a master's from the Naval War College in National Security and Strategic Studies.

After retiring from the Navy in 2014, Jim traded his flight suit for leadership roles in change management, aviation management, and emergency management at the same major California utility company he still works for today.

These days, he and his amazing wife, Sarah, split their home time between the Bay area and Kona, Hawaii. When they're not working, you'll find them traveling the globe, SCUBA diving, and collecting life experiences the way some people collect fridge magnets.

www.ingramcontent.com/pod-product-compliance
Lightning Source LLC
Chambersburg PA
CBHW060140130626
46556CB00006B/2429